GAIL FORREST

ALLINED BOOKS · PENNSYLVANIA

GONEPAUSAL

Copyright © 2018 Gail Forrest

www.gonepausal.com

All rights reserved. No part of this book may be reproduced or transmitted in any form or by any means, electronic or mechanical, including photocopying, recording, or by any information storage and retrieval system, without permission in writing from the publisher.

Published by Allined Books

For information: www.allinedbooks.com

Printed in the United States of America

Acknowledgements

SINCE I PROBABLY WILL NEVER WIN an Academy Award, this is my pretend acceptance speech.

I want to thank my mother who thinks I'm smart and funny, my friend Neil who first believed in *gonepausal* as a book, my dog Potato who sat patiently and watched me write instead of take him for a walk, my agent Laurie who also thinks I'm funny but very bad at punctuation, my son Jesse for not caring if he had home-cooked meals, all my internet dates without whom I would not still be single or have dating blogs, and my friends who took my phone calls all these years without procuring restraining orders—you know who you are!

Thank you.

Introduction

I DIDN'T KNOW WHAT TO EXPECT from menopause. I'd heard the word many times but had no idea the effect it would have on me psychologically and physically. The closest I got to tales from the menopause front was overhearing two of my clients at an art fair in New York City who were both in their late 50s, laughing about their lack of a sex drive. They caught me eavesdropping, pulled me aside and gave me a secret glimpse into the future. I was in my early forties so their words seemed meaningless instead of prophetic.

"Just wait until you reach menopause, you'll have no interest in sex either," Sandra smirked.

I distinctly remember thinking, never! That will never happen to me. It may have happened to the two of you but it will not be me. I felt smug and impervious to their predictions. It was a moment I would always remember. That was all I ever learned about menopause.

I was ambushed, as menopause affects every woman. It caught up with me, regardless of my determination to be different. There was no escape, detour, magic potion or way to expedite the process. Until recently, it has been every woman for herself because it was rarely discussed. My mother never said a word. It appeared to be a very hush hush subject. Bodily changes were a forbidden subject to her generation. Did they all take a vow of silence?

The baby boomer women are much more audacious, and prepared to talk. We definitely want to know what the hell is going on with our body and mind. Why am I laughing one minute and sobbing the next? Why are my keys in the refrigerator? Do my glasses have legs?

Disturbingly, my clients were right, as my desire to have sex is #10 on my to-do list, right after vacuuming my car. I have kissed my dewy complexion goodbye because the loss of estrogen sucked the youth right off my cheeks. I repeat, what the hell happened? I needed answers and a better sense of humor.

After I had a baby, I told every one of my pregnant friends the truth; it hurts like hell and there is no way to be prepared. I felt it was ridiculous to sugarcoat it. I believe menopause is similar. Women need to guide each other through this life phase, not be afraid to say what's on their minds. We need to maintain a sense of humor about this personal sea change.

Gonepausal is a cranky, funny way of looking at this time of life. The medically-based books provide helpful information about physical symptoms but if you can't laugh about hot flashes, forgetfulness, lack of a sex drive, dry lifeless skin tone, exhaustion, disappearing glasses, missing cell phones and feeling pissed off, there's no way to get through this no matter how much scientific information you gather. So hang on and enjoy the ride.

CONTENTS

	ACKNOWLEDGEMENTS	iii
	INTRODUCTION	v
1	WHINE-OH	1
	The Pause that Refreshes?	2
	Requiem for a Laptop	5
	Has Anyone Seen My Glasses?	8
	Deodorant, Tampax, Condoms and Vibrators, Oh My	10
	You're Never Too Old to be Ten Again	13
	Get Me to the Ashram, Not the Nunnery	16
	High School vs. Menopause	18
	Seattle, Salmon, Andy and Luis, Oh My!	20
	Big Pharma and Little Me	23
	Everything Must Go Go Go!	26
	Outsmarted by My Phone	28
	Wedding Announcements Can Ruin a Perfectly Nice Sunday	30
	Have You Seen My Password?	32
	I Have a Teeny Tiny Stalker	34
	I "Out-Carried" Carrie Bradshaw	36
	Peeing in a Cup: A Tragic Female Dilemma	41
	Jewish Princess Blues	43
	Ninety-Five Year Old Man Looking for a Hookup	45
	Sex or the Internet?	48
	Don't Call Me, I'll Call You	50
	Who Are the People in People?	52

2   REALLY! 55

"Mirror, Mirror on the Wall, That Can't Be Me" 56

"Bathrobe Woman" vs. My Bank Account 58

Dad, Poor Dad, I've Caught Him Watching Porn and I'm Feeling So Sad 60

I Confess: I Am Not "Hip" Anymore 63

I Hate The New Yorker 65

I'm Calling a Cab 67

Mid-Fork a Tarnished Romance 70

Studying the Tribal Women of Orange County 73

Don't Grow Old with Me 75

Girls, Uncle Sam Wants You! 77

Bye-Bye Rio 79

"For Richer or for Richer" 81

Relationship "Deal Breakers" or Living Alone 83

Baby Boomers, Be Afraid, Be Very Afraid... and Don't Watch TV 86

Help! My House is Surrounded by the Starbucks Police! 88

Labor Day or Laborious Day? 90

I Hate Packing Boxes! 92

Home Alone 94

Blue M&Ms 96

"Princess Stripped of Crown!" or I Hate to Shop 98

I Paid $38 for a Dinner Roll 101

Let Me Eat Cake 104

To Tattoo or Not to Tattoo? 107

Valentine's Day vs. New Year's Eve 109

Bad Date Hall of Fame Awards 111

3 WHERE? 115

Lounge Lizards and Me *116*

"No, No. Anything but the Car Keys!" *120*

What's so Happy about Happy Hour? *122*

Bye-bye Bergdorfs *124*

I Abdicated my Throne for a Bowl of Chili *126*

National Holidays Got You Down? Eat Pez and Drink *129*

This Blonde Didn't Have More Fun *131*

I'll Have What She's Having *133*

Men on Sale at Match.com *135*

Bedroom Crime Scene *138*

I Feel Better About My Face, Neck and Finances! *140*

Sex, Prunes and the Sahara *143*

I like Wine and to Whine *145*

No Cooking Required *147*

Queen of One Date Tells All *149*

Call 911 and Get a Husband! *152*

First Read The Manual! *154*

Sex and the Elephant *156*

Little Bo Peep and Her Sleep Deprived Sheep *158*

I Hate Reality TV More than The New Yorker *160*

Face Down *162*

My New Life of Dating Guppies *164*

4   FACE VALUE 167

Win $3,000, a Trip to Paris, or Me.. 168

"I Do...At Least I Think I Do" 172

Woodstock—The Wonder Years... 174

I Climbed Mt Everest in My Kate Spade High Heels............... 176

Right on, Mom!... 179

I Am Not a Bar Loser Anymore 181

A Little Dab'll Do Ya... 184

R.I.P My Prada Purse 186

I Look Better in Dim Lighting 189

Collecting Husbands and Stamps 191

My First Kiss: Fact or Fiction?.. 194

Fractured Fairy Tale 196

Prune Danish 199

I Want a Dog's Life... 201

Why I Am Not a Cougar 203

I Feel Bad About My Face and Neck...................................... 205

KISS ME! But Only if You Can 207

Me and the Prince of Denmark.. 209

Botox or Bust?.. 211

Ken Dolls Grow Old, Too 213

Dressing for Successful Dating.. 215

Dance of the Seven Plungers!.. 218

I Need a Push-up Bra... 221

I.
Whine-Oh

The Pause that Refreshes?

WHEN IT CAME TO MENOPAUSE, my girlfriends and I were confused. We were never sure which of us was 'peri-' and which was '-pausal.' Are they two distinctly different experiences or one long, drawn-out holding cell and then you die? Would I ever remember my sister's phone number again? Would I stop bursting into tears when my running shoes came untied?

According to my gynecologist, my skin would be a sign I have moved on from the peri- part. His prophecy of a dry lifeless complexion was mind numbing. He swears he can tell every woman in his waiting room who has gone through menopause by her skin tone. I tested myself, stared around at the dewy complexions of the pregnant beauties, and burst into tears. I decided to get a new doctor.

A good resource about how menopause will affect you is your mother, as genetic predisposition is a key factor. Since my mom and I never had the birds and bees talk, I really didn't know how we were going to dig into menopause. She was from the generation of women who repressed everything related to sex and bodily functions. (I have noticed however, much like Gandhi at the end of his life she is now obsessed with bodily functions.)

I decided to raise the topic over a casual dinner, somewhere between her complaining that the salmon smelled funny and that my sister never calls. I decided since we were in conversational free fall, why not.

"So Mother, I was wondering, how old do you think you were when you went through menopause? How long did it take? What did you feel like? Did you feel anxious and totally forgetful like me? How about hot flashes? Sometimes? Never?" I know my rapid fire questioning might have been overwhelming but I was on a roll. I was nervously tapping my knife on the table, keeping rhythm with my questions. Maybe I asked too many, for starters.

I *should* mention that my mother is an overachiever and quite competitive. A college graduate long before women earned degrees, she speaks three languages, has been a guest on the Phil Donahue Show and has testified before the U.S. Senate on vocational education. She doesn't like to be upstaged by anyone.

There we were at this defining moment in mother/daughter relations, passing the torch kind of stuff. She put down her fork, took the napkin from her lap and rested it on the table, and quite casually said, "I went through menopause in one afternoon. Dessert?"

Requiem for a Laptop

2018 WAS NOT EVEN 12 HOURS OLD when disaster struck. I abandoned any thoughts of my New Year's resolutions earlier than planned and switched into a state of high anxiety.

The day had started out innocently enough; I dragged my sleepy, sorry self to my desk and turned on my laptop. It just sat there dark and dead as a doornail. Sweating, I screamed, "Why won't you start?" I stared intensely at the little machine as if magically I could will it on. Ever so slowly, it flickered into existence but then wouldn't connect to the internet. I plugged and unplugged every cord connected to the metal box. I did a virus check. I defragged. I have no idea what that meant but it sounded crucial. I clicked on all the icons that looked helpful and then I went searching for a baseball bat. "Work or die!" I yelled.

I was in techno-meltdown. I was short of breath and patience. I didn't know what I needed first: drugs, a martini, an emergency room or Bill Gates. My friend Dennis tried to calm me down and suggested I take it to Best Buy for a checkup. "Checkup? I think it needs life support," I cried as I grabbed my laptop and hightailed it to the car. As a punishment, I was tempted to tie it to the bumper and drag it behind me. Thankfully, even in my psycho state I knew that might feel purging but was counter-productive. I ran into the store mowing down everyone in my path. "Heads up, I have a dying laptop."

I threw the computer and myself on the Geek Squad counter and burst into tears. "Help me Geek man; I can't get on the internet. My Dell is trying to die."

He ignored my histrionics and looked at the machine with consideration. "Ma'am this laptop is at least 5 years old." Uh oh, that sounded fatal. "Have you ever changed the battery or AC cord?"

"No," I blushed in my techno-ignorance.

"Well you should have by now. You could try that and we could give it a thorough checkup but that's a Band-Aid and not a cure."

Not a cure? I needed a cure, a vaccine, a pill, a transplant.

"I suggest you're better off putting the money in a new laptop."

I think I lost consciousness. "New...computer," I stuttered, as I felt the room start to spin.

"Yes Ma'am."

I wasn't ready to let my little Dell go; it was my first. A new computer might make my head explode. I learned how to copy and paste on this one. I finally figured out the paper clip symbol stands for "attach" and I can actually do it without crying. Only last week I learned you could have more than one window open at a time.

Is there liturgy and proper funerary clothing for a laptop at the end? And how long after its death is it appropriate to buy a new one? More importantly, will my neighbors come with casseroles?

Has Anyone Seen My Glasses?

MY GLASSES HAVE VANISHED. Gone, I say! I know they couldn't just up and walk away. Glasses can't walk, right? Even worse, they were expensive. Tragically, I looked bad in every single pair except the $400 frames. I call them my "no more vacations" glasses. Now I can't see and the trip to Florida is off.

I looked in the washing machine and dryer; no glasses. But I did find a blue hat that wasn't mine, and my missing running shoe. Nope, not in the dishwasher either (which I should unload soon). My glasses were dirty so that actually was a reasonable option. I ripped apart the couch, which I don't advise unless your dog is the same color as the fabric. I haven't used the oven in six months but after my usual two glasses of wine, it was a possibility.

But wait, they must be in my purse. I ravaged it at least four times and vowed never again to buy one with so many compartments. They didn't turn up in the box with my new

Kate Spade high heels, but it did make me long for a place to wear them, and also question why I bought them. The refrigerator was a bust but I am in desperate need of food and no wonder I'm always hungry. The garbage made sense, yet no. Under the bed, behind the bed, nope and nope. I promised, however, to vacuum before the week was up. A lightbulb went off! They might be in a jacket pocket. I was crazed and sweating when I concluded I had too many pockets, or can you never have enough? Why was the dog now staring at me? Did he eat the glasses because there's no homework?

The car, they absolutely had to be in the car, as I need them to drive. Glove compartment, trunk, under the driver's seat, passenger seat, between the seats, cup holders—nothing resembling glasses, but I wondered if the Snickers bar wedged in the back was still edible. No glasses, only the crazy realization that this is my new "normal."

Deodorant, Tampax, Condoms and Vibrators, Oh My

EVERYONE'S BEEN EMBARRASSED. It's embarrassing. Thankfully, I've outgrown blushing, as that added insult to injury. My face appearing like it was tomato red and about to explode was not a good look for me.

As I've grown older, the things about which I want to die a thousand deaths have changed. When I was a preteen, I would perspire profusely in my pretty party dresses at boy/girl parties. This was a particularly nasty sight when I was wearing light purple. I would sweat down to my waist, run in fright to the blow dryer in the bathroom and stand under it until all traces of perspiration were gone. Sometimes I'd miss the slow dances, which was the only reason I went. I tried Mitchum deodorant as it was supposed to block my sweat glands. I figured I would either die from toxic buildup or make it through a party without ruining my dress. Luckily, I've outgrown this problem.

As if sweating wasn't bad enough, the next life embarrassment was buying Tampax. It was a badge of honor and a source of horror. If there were a boy in the store who could see me buying the highly identifiable blue box, I'd hang out in the candy aisle until he left. Sometimes this took 20 minutes of my standing around reading the ingredients on a Snickers bar.

Another embarrassing product is condoms. At the moment, being single, my menopausal sex life is actually on pause so no condoms required. Although I do remember standing for an hour staring at the choices: Lubricated, medicated, intoxicated, flavored, hypoallergenic, hallucinogenic, candy coated, colored, ribbed and satin smooth. The deliberation gave me a headache, which actually solved my problem and I went home.

I just read I can now buy a vibrator at my local CVS, Walgreens or Walmart. It's more convenient than finding a cute little sex toy boutique but a lot more public. "Attention CVS shoppers, woman wearing North Face parka in Aisle 6 opening all the vibrator boxes." Excuse me, how else can you actually know what they look like?

There is one more product that has put the tomato red back on my face—shopping for vaginal lubrication, or as I like to call it, WD40. Without hormones, I describe sex as a sandpaper experience. There was no moaning in delight, just screaming in pain. It is embarrassing to be standing in front of all the lubrication options and trying to decide which will take the "coarse" out of intercourse. I like to be alone in the aisle. My friend Karen told me about a product that works surprisingly well called "Slippery Stuff" and thankfully comes in handy little packets or containers you can slip in your purse in case the moment arises and you're not home. Ironically, regardless of when the moment arises there really is not much spontaneity in having to pull out lubricating gel.

You never really outgrow embarrassment.

You're Never Too Old to be Ten Again

OUCH! OUCH! AND OMG ARE YOU FREAKING KIDDING ME? How and why are women submitting to what seems to be the "extreme sport" of beauty? It's crazy to me why anyone would want to become prepubescent all over again. It was hard enough when I was wishing and hoping for breasts, obsessing that I would never have a reason to trade my little white undershirts for a bra. To say nothing of the nightmare of wearing anklets before my mother let me shave my legs. I felt doomed to a life in my bedroom. After all, I couldn't go to a boy/girl party looking more primate than Homo sapiens. Ah, the wonderful childhood memories of hairy legs and a flat chest.

Now decades later on the horizon lies a question I could never have imagined.

To Brazilian or not to Brazilian, and am I really asking myself this question? Incidentally, I don't mean a trip to Rio, or a good strong cup of coffee. I am also not talking about the ridiculously expensive but gloriously humidity defying Brazilian Blowout, which, btw, my hair could use right now. Oh no, I am talking about the bikini wax gone rogue, the mother of all waxes, the kill me now waxing of all pubic hair. Whose idea was this? Is Kate Moss behind the conspiracy; she looks oddly hairless. Decades after going through puberty, I should now consider looking 10-years-old again?

Surprisingly, it was a man who told me about this new beauty regimen and yes, I was dating him. "You talkin' to me Mister?" I became weak, sweaty and oddly itchy. A mind-numbing bikini wax isn't enough?

Consensus, I desperately needed consensus! Was every woman hairless? Did I miss the memo? Is this the new normal? I needed data quick! I collected answers from my male inner circle regardless of my burning desire to ask every man and woman I saw in Starbucks. A nonfat grande mocha skim latte or Brazilian wax?

Data is a mixed blessing. From my male friends I heard two words more associated with aviation than a beauty must—landing strip and runway. I wasn't deterred by my visual confusion or urge to book a vacation as I queried my women friends. Oddly, they were less adventurous and not venturing further north than a bikini wax. Trying not to get arrested, I looked around the locker room at the gym. Whew, filled with women afraid to fly.

Is a sign a "sign?" I saw plastered in the window of a beauty salon: "Brazilian Waxing Special 30% off on Regular Price. $50 now $35. Only Tuesday."

It was Wednesday.

Get Me to the Ashram, Not the Nunnery

MY FRIEND RICK THINKS I'M SOUNDING "GROUCHY." I wonder if that's his nice way of saying that I've become a raving bitch. I am getting a little cranky. I'm sick and tired of trying to figure out if I have enough money for the rest of my life, which could be a really long time because my mom is 100. I need advice but in reality, I definitely need more money.

To add insult to crankiness, the health care debates are actually starting to give me hives, so should I or shouldn't I call a doctor? My nerves are shattered and who's going to refill my Xanax? I need peace, love and 1966. Get me to an ashram or yoga retreat ASAP. I read the places are bulging at the seams with cranky folk just like me. I want my bestie Adria to stop jumping up and down on her computer keyboard over her stressful job and join me. We need quiet—shhhhhhh—and cheap room and board.

I could meditate. I read that at the Himalayan Institute's 28-day self-transformation program, the day begins with

6:00 a.m. meditation. Excuse me? I couldn't possibly start self-transformation that early. I can't begin transforming until 10:30 after three cups of coffee and a quick application of eye shadow and more recently, I've had to add mascara. The day continues with Hatha yoga classes, breathing and relaxation practicum, and about four hours of light chores like making beds and chopping vegetables. What the f**k is a "practicum?" As for "light" chores, those aren't light!

I feel crankiness returning. I hate making beds and absolutely do not do "hospital corners." I throw the covers over the pillows. I also don't want to chop. Do I look like Anthony Bourdain? I'm starting to itch again.

I need different chores, like selecting a nice Sauvignon Blanc for dinner. Oh and I don't share, so no bunking with others. And definitely my own bathroom; I am absolutely non-negotiable on this. I am a bathroom reader so I wonder if I could forward my New York Times subscription.

OM! I feel more relaxed already. Maybe just thinking about self-transformation and meditation is good enough. Now where did I put the mascara?

High School vs. Menopause

I CANNOT DECIDE IF HIGH SCHOOL WAS WORSE than being menopausal. They both shocked me into a new reality. The transition from the quiet safety of middle school to the pressure-packed halls of high school with the emotionally draining pressure of grades and clothes, or the turmoil of menopause with my sex drive in reverse, pasty dry complexion and constant search for my keys or glasses. Hard to pick which was more mind-altering.

At New Trier High School, we had the unwritten "one-week" rule—no repeat outfits for one week. Talk about anxiety. I wasn't great at mixing and matching so by Thursday I was a nervous wreck and declared I was sick and had to stay home.

I probably have better things to do than ruminate about A-line skirts and cable knit sweaters, but I just had three of my girlfriends from high school visit and it was like we were back in 1966. First and foremost, we were convinced we all looked exactly the same. No one noticed wrinkled foreheads, deepened nasolabial folds or gained weight. We saw each other as our high school selves. Barbara had kept her assignment notebook from sophomore year and we recreated each and every day. We were very shallow. Birthdays, half birthdays, parties, driving around aimlessly and boys filled every waking hour. We all got into college but I have no idea how, given our busy schedules. I am, however, convinced Barbara was invited to more sweet sixteen parties than I was which is disturbing. I am still shallow.

I was also surprised at how many boys we mixed and matched like Villager outfits. They were a huge part of our thought process or our only thought. Some relationships lasted three days, others two weeks and why Bill dropped me is still a mystery. It set me back most of freshman year. Thankfully, Dave asked me out behind his cheerleader girlfriend's back and I recovered. Shallow but happy again.

Our lunch lasted five hours, yet felt way too short. There's no end to reliving the times we shared. I liked being in 1966 again. I have to confess however I don't look exactly the same; my hair's shorter, I have a furrowed brow, nasolabial folds and a neck that looks more like my dad's every day. High school may be an anxiety-filled memory but not the friends that I carried with me.

Seattle, Salmon, Andy and Luis, Oh My!

IT HAPPENED. I thought technology was impervious to death. I thought I had purchased a "til death do us part" cell phone, yet not exactly. It lay limp in my hand no matter what I pushed or banged. To top it off, I was completely frazzled after driving virtually non-stop with my son from Chicago to Seattle in order to get him to his medical residency on schedule. I was sleep deprived, hungry, and still shaking after a storm almost blew the car into Canada. And now my little phone was DOA in my hotel room. I burst into tears and threw myself on the bed in a fit of despair. Why me? Why now? Why when all I wanted was a piece of Pacific salmon?

I was soaking wet and in a towel when I made this shocking discovery. I can't live without a cell phone. It's the 21st century; I need to communicate 24/7. I found myself screaming, "I hate you," at the dead object. After I regained sanity, I grabbed a pair of my ratty gym shorts that are never supposed to be worn in public, pink flip flops, the shredded t-shirt I sleep in and ran down to the lobby, dressing as I went. All bets of propriety and decency were off.

The concierge found the nearest AT&T store for me after I promised to finish putting on my clothes. I jumped in a cab clutching my old cell. "I never dropped you! I kept you dry and away from large bodies of water, and this is what I get?"

I crossed two lanes of traffic and ran into the phone store, throwing myself on the mercy of the man behind the counter. Luis was calm and thankfully didn't have me taken away in an ambulance.

"Help me Luis! I need my phone numbers, my messages, SALMON!" He was so patient and I was so nuts.

An hour later, I left the store with a shiny red phone, a pile of rebate paperwork and his card. He sweetly told me to come back if I needed assistance, as he'd be available nightly until 7:00.

I loved my new phone. It was sleek and had a lot of useless options. Most importantly, I was back in the world of 24-hour communication. Except the phone got hotter and hotter and hotter every time I used it. I felt like my hand was going to catch on fire. Was my little red phone a "weapon of mass destruction"?

I hightailed it back to Luis at 6:45 the next night. 'Andy' was at my guy Luis's desk.

"Where's Luis?" I cried. I need him; he promised he'd be here until 7:00."

"Luis had to go home to his wife," Andy calmly responded as he watched me sweat and pace.

"But what about me," I whined.

Who cared about his wife, it wasn't 7:00 yet! Andy patiently heard the tale of my little red "WMD," nodding patronizingly. He nicely took the phone from my hand and replaced it with a new silver model.

"Can you set it up like Luis did?" I pleaded.

But Andy was on to me. "I bet you're pretty good at getting people to do things for you. I know your type." Hmm, little Andy must have been a psychology major. He was right but I liked him anyway.

I'd been in Seattle for two days. I had two new cell phones, two men who I thank for not calling the paramedics and no salmon.

Big Pharma and Little Me

HELP ME, I'M AN ADDICT, a main-liner, wide-eyed, shaking and itchy waiting for my next fix. Get those commercials about Viagra off my screen, as who has time for sex when there is 24/7 BREAKING NEWS? And geez has it ever been more addicting? Come on, what's happening now makes my Watergate years seem like "Introduction to Scandal 101." It's the big time, baby. As terrified as I am of needles, I have stuck the news needle in my arm and there is no emergency number to call or a quick fix. Ironically, there is a drug that can save you from a heroin overdose, but has Big Pharma come up with one for my addiction—no! Come on pharmaceutical boys, I need an antidote.

I admit I was in a weakened state; fatigue had set in after 16 months on the campaign trail. And feeling so certain my girl would triumph, the plunge to her political death almost sent me to the ER. Shock and dismay, I'd say. I sulked around in funerary attire for weeks and ate copious amounts of

Oreos, which did not lessen my sadness but did ruin a perfectly good complexion. I slapped myself into political alert after the inauguration. Why was I licking my wounds and eating cookies when I should be safeguarding the country by watching news shows all day? Dusk 'til dawn talking heads and the mind numbing, brain cell-killing scroll at the bottom of the screen.

I have too many friends now to keep track of: Brian Williams, Anderson Cooper, Van Jones (isn't he a hottie?), Don Lemon, David Gergen, Rachel Maddow, the ever enigmatic Greta Van Susteren (bi-political in my estimation) and scads of others. To say nothing of my personal spy operation over at FOX—very deep throat.

I have learned that news isn't always news but fake. Who would have guessed there's an alternative to reality without dropping acid? And what ever happened to "no news is good news?" There is no such thing; I'm bombarded every waking moment like a rapid-fire machine gun. Obamacare, TrumpCare (he doesn't really care), Russian interference, pipelines, tax cuts, North Korea, China, wall building (Mexico is never paying), Darth Vader (aka Steve Bannon), more military, less NPR. This is what my poor, addled brain wakes up to and yet I lunge for the remote even before caffeine.

I have searched the internet for a local exorcist to come free me of addiction, as I fear a man of the clergy would be useless in this area. Big Pharma call me.

Everything Must Go Go Go!

COME ONE, COME ALL! Come on down. I've decided to pay off my VISA bill so all the clothes in my closet are for sale. That's right—everything—and not just the nice stuff. It's an "everything must go" blowout. Clothes for all seasons. Most of them are clean, except my parka, that's a little nasty unless you like horses and yellow Labrador retrievers. I also have a "dressy" down jacket for that special evening out. It's black, it's puffy, it's warm and it has a "North Face" logo. Nothing says, "I'm special" like a logo. To make this purchase even better I'll throw in, at no extra charge, the slightly dirty mittens that are stuffed in the pockets. You heard it right and you heard it here.

If you love black, I'm your closet. I have dresses, skirts, sweaters, coats, jackets, belts, t-shirts and bras, all black. Say good-bye to color and come on over. Here's another reason to shop with me and not at Neimans; I'm serving cocktails 24/7. Yep, even the champagne you've been craving but are too cheap to order. I do, however, have a strict "you stain it, you own it" policy.

Hate to dress up and looking for something more casual? For one day only, I'm willing to part with my old shabby "New York Sports Club" gym shorts and my ripped beyond recognition, 1986 New York Mets World Series t-shirt. Either item must go to a loving home.

To sweeten the sale even further, I will be spraying Estee Lauder's "Beautiful" perfume on the first 50 customers. If it's good enough for Gwyneth Paltrow… and besides, then you'll get that Saks feeling and forget you're in a closet.

Better hurry, I'm getting a little anxious and starting to rethink this incredible offer. And in your rush to get here don't forget it's a cash only closet.

Outsmarted by My Phone

I CONFESS. MY NEW SMARTPHONE IS SMARTER THAN I AM. It's true, no contest. Hands down, the phone wins. It doesn't matter that I went to college, was an English major and read a lot of books. Symbolism, metaphors, similes and allegory have nothin' on my new shiny Galaxy S5. It doesn't care that Moby Dick wasn't just a whale, or poor Hester Prynne had to wear a scarlet letter, or whether or not it was "the best or worst of times." Nope, the horrid little machine has made a mockery of me. My brain is full of the wrong information. And all these years I thought I was smart. I'm so over.

Admittedly, the pressure to possess a smartphone had become too great. I was laughed at by my peer group, and even children under 12, because I didn't have one. I began to feel unpopular which reminded me I wasn't picked for the cheerleading squad in high school, although years of therapy helped.

Truthfully, I was happy with my not-so-smart phone. It had a keyboard that was like a typewriter, not the surface of a skating rink like my new device. My typing skills are useless as I miss every letter and have now resigned myself to the new spelling of my name—"Fsuj." I have yet to figure out how to answer the phone and simply stare at it when it rings. As for all the pictures I planned on taking and sending to friends and family—not happening. I saw myself in the viewfinder by mistake and needed a Valium. I can swipe the screen and find technological happiness according to the critics. Who are these people and shouldn't they get out more?

I have one more day to decide the fate of my Galaxy S5 and whether or not we have a future. Tomorrow is the return deadline. The folks at the Verizon store hide in the back when they see me, as I now spend all my free time there begging for help and counseling. I feel like the techno Hamlet: "To return or not to return?" I believe my friend Gregg has a Vegas line going on the fate of the phone.

Call me ASAP if you think you can help; but then again I don't know how to answer.

Wedding Announcements Can Ruin a Perfectly Nice Sunday

DO YOU WANT TO FEEL REALLY BAD ABOUT YOURSELF, and not only yourself but your children? Read the bridal announcements in the Sunday New York Times; you'll definitely feel self-loathing.

Every week it makes me crazy; who are these people? Reading about the brides, grooms and their parents could send me to therapy or a bar. Each bride or groom has saved the lives of hundreds of homeless people by the age of 20, climbed Mt. Everest more than once, earned a Ph.D. in English and Microbiology, created a software program during their senior year at an Ivy League school and sold it for $50 million, lived in a tent in the Sub-Sahara tending to drought victims or is "on track" to be the youngest Senator in U.S. history. Who does this?

It gets worse. The parents of these wunderkind are weapons of ego destruction. Both mother and father alike have cured some form of cancer, discovered a new gene therapy that will eradicate all diseases that start with the letter "M," produced seven Oscar winning movies, run the campaigns of three presidents, written a Pulitzer Prize winning novel which was turned into a film that grossed $300 million, helped get Nelson Mandela released from prison, or know Oprah. I have weekly feelings of failure and throw the bridal section in the garbage without bothering to recycle. I'm frantic, need medication and definitely more education.

I have one grown son so I have to prepare my list of accomplishments soon. I've wracked my brain as to what I could proclaim in the paper. So far I've come up with: worked selling shoes for a day, candy striper for one semester senior year in high school (with pictures to prove it), grocery store check-out girl at 16 but that could have been my sister, pizza waitress for 4 hours and 15 minutes in college, waited tables for one lunch hour shift after college, changes the oil every 3,000 miles and in 2009 learned to "copy and paste" on a laptop.

I have six days until the next wedding announcements are released and my ego is tested once again. That's not even enough time to get to the base camp of Mt. Everest.

Have You Seen My Password?

I WAS READY TO PULL MY HAIR OUT, run around the house screaming or throw myself on the bed sobbing. On second thought, I'd hate to ruin my hair as I just paid a fortune to get it cut. Running and screaming is a real possibility, as is sobbing. What could drive me to such mania? I can't remember the password for my MacBook. I felt on the verge of password insanity. I know I wrote it down on the notepad I brought to my last lesson at the Apple store. One of the Apple boy toys and I reset my password and I specifically jotted it down so as not to forget it. Ironically and tragically, I forgot where I put the damn pad. I've ripped my desk apart three times and nada. I just tore through every compartment in my car and zippo. I did find the lipstick I was looking for, however, which is a relief and it is still a good color for me.

I am sick of this password world. Whose idea was all these codes? I need to blame someone, anyone or everyone. I've tried every combination of words I can think of to get into my MacBook. It does this crazy little shimmy shake denying me access.

"Let me in, it's me, you stupid little white box! I hate you!"

I'm out of control and developing a nasty, itchy rash on my cheek. Now I have no computer access and need a dermatologist. Sobbing seems more and more like a good plan. I find myself longing for the days of envelopes, stamps and good penmanship.

Alas, my afternoon will be spent in the bright white Apple store at the mercy and schedule of the boys at the Genius Bar. "Oh little brainiac boy disciples of Steven Jobs, help me find my way. I'm lost again, need your guidance and more importantly your pity."

I'd like to just throw my MacBook at the wall and hope that would trigger its memory. Although that would feel cathartic, I stop to scratch my rash and think better of it. Once again, I am reminded of the fact that I am a computer loser. With my head bowed in dismay, I tuck the MacBook under my arm and head out into the big bad world to find my password.

I Have a Teeny Tiny Stalker

I'M BEING FOLLOWED. YES, IT'S TRUE; someone is after me. It's weird and also unnerving. However, I no longer check under the bed or in my closet like I did when I was a little girl and was certain there was someone waiting to "get" me the minute I closed my eyes.

Every morning when I wake up my stalker is there. Each day, the first thing I do is drag my sleepy, sorry ass to my computer to check my emails, hoping against hope for some fun or riveting correspondence. Instead there she is, waiting like clockwork. POOF! On my screen appears yet another message from "The Bra Genie.com." I'd prefer she was in a bottle rather than my laptop. Hmmm. I wonder if she's in cahoots with my mother. No, Mom likes to work alone.

I have no idea how the pesky nymph got my email address. Could she be in partnership with "Window Replacement. com," a company that also pops up in my emails and for some reason thinks I own a window? "I rent!" I yell at the screen.

No, the Bra Genie is much more persistent and obviously knows me a lot better. "It's true, little Genie. I need bras, but what scares me is, how did you find out?" I've tried on bras in every lingerie department from Neimans to Target. I'm a bra tire kicker. I've left dressing rooms piled with them in a myriad of colors, sizes and styles. They looked nice on the hanger but pinched, itched, or rode up. "No, no and no," I've told countless sales ladies who shook their heads in despair and confusion as I marched out of the store empty handed. No bra for me. I long for the bras I burned back in the late sixties as I think those actually fit, to say nothing of how a bra costs as much as a Honda now.

I couldn't wait to wear a bra when I was a young girl. I didn't care if I needed one or not, I just had to get out of undershirts. Now I'm a grown up and "The Bra Genie" plagues me with the promise of comfort, no slip straps and six for the price of three. "Get back in a damn bottle where you belong, little creature, and bring me Aladdin with a lamp and three wishes—none of which will be for a bra but one might be for a Honda."

I "Out-Carried" Carrie Bradshaw

I "OUT-CARRIED" CARRIE BRADSHAW. Yep, I have left Carrie in the dust. I admit I could never compete with her in the shoe department or was ever brave enough to wear some of her crazy looking outfits but now at long last Carrie has nothing on me in the break-up arena. I can now declare myself the winner and probably long-term champion of ways in which to be dumped. I remember the poor girl's plight when she woke up to a breakup Post-it note from her boyfriend, Berger. Oh no, not a Post-it! Who does that? Who steals off in the wee hours of the morning leaving a tiny yellow piece of paper that reads, "I can't do this." A slam-dunk of a breakup, I'd say.

It left a pit in my stomach as I swore at him on my TV screen. "You're an asshole; who does such a heartless, cowardly thing?"

My heart went out to her, as our little Carrie was stunned and sickened by the short and hideous content stuck to her kitchen cabinet. My girl was in tears, not knowing how it went so wrong so quickly. Only 12 hours earlier, they were a happy couple and then presto-chango a Post-it stated they were over. It left me with a small rash yet incredibly relieved it was a TV show and not real life.

Real life is so much worse. I didn't meet the young, hot, groovy Berger; I met a 72-year old man with hair, which is pretty much a perk past the age of 55. He was in decent shape, which translates into his stomach didn't hang too far over his belt. He was smart, had a great laugh and seemed to love being in my company. He followed me like a sweet, odd puppy looking for home. My Berger just wanted to do what I wanted to do when he wasn't golfing. We ate, drank and seemed pretty damn merry. He grew on me as we laughed at the same things, had a similar quirky outlook on life and he gave me piggyback rides, which is a real deal closer for me.

While I ordered wine at dinner on date two, he talked about sex. Did I like sex? Did I want to have sex? When were we going to have sex—today, tomorrow, the next day? *When* was the operative question. I should have called a cab.

Of course I liked sex, I was a girl of the 1970s. I was a bra burner, a hippie chick who appreciated a hot guy with a great pony tail and good weed. Was my 72-year old Berger shittin' me? But more importantly why was he obsessed with the subject? Shouldn't he be worried about his cholesterol or cataracts? And why didn't I stick to my "we need to know each other better" rule? He wiggled his way into my life with words like "I'm absolutely crazy about you," "you make me happy," "you're good for me" and the phrase-de-resistance "I have never had such a great time with anyone." Zing went my heartstrings.

    I did what Carrie would have done—had sex. First time sex after the age of 55 does not resemble 29-year old sex. Scrambling for Viagra and Astroglide does not beg spontaneity. I'm hoping he doesn't turn blue or have to be hospitalized with an erection that lasts more than four hours, and he's complaining about the greasy lotion ruining his Egyptian cotton sheets. And getting a first look at a 72-year old male body can also set back eroticism until the shock wears off. It definitely makes me rethink the notion of senior citizen chemistry.

    What are these old guys talking about in their insistence on this magical state—have they looked in the mirror lately? You might say having sex is like riding a bike, except your fancy 10-speed has turned into a rusty old Schwinn. Sex does not get better with age but if given time and caring it can be warmer, more intimate and wonderful. My old Berger didn't have time, no matter how "absolutely crazy" he was about me or how "happy" I made him. Time was not on my side.

While I thought our sex life was improving with every attempt, he must have been thinking it was falling short of internet porn, which I think is the new standard by which women must perform. Not being an aficionado of these sites, I had no idea what my competition was and if I could possibly measure up. I never had a chance. My affection for him was growing with each date and I knew that good sex was on the horizon. But my 72-year old Berger had no interest in "growing affection"—he was on the hunt for a porn girl. I have to repeat, "has he looked in the mirror lately?" If so, it's the magic kind.

The rest of our relationship ironically was magic. We cracked each other up, and actually ran around town like two adolescents ditching school. I hadn't had that much outright fun with anyone in years. If only I had a dollar for every time he told me how "absolutely crazy" he was about me, I could have bought a pair of Carrie's fabulous Manolos. I was happy and unprepared.

It was a Tuesday at 4:45 when I got a text from old Berger. He often texted me sweet messages during the day so expecting another cute note I hurriedly clicked to read it.

"I am absolutely crazy about you but want to break up."

Take that Carrie Bradshaw! I got you good. Much like Carrie, I practically stumbled to my knees. I was ambushed by my 72-year old Berger with the 21st century Post-it—a text.

I could go on and tell you about the subsequent phone call but it's pointless as the message said it all. My heart was broken. The only consolation was realizing I had "out-Carried" Carrie Bradshaw.

Peeing in a Cup: A Tragic Female Dilemma

IT'S REALLY HARD TO PEE IN A CUP. If there's a trick to it, I'm clueless. This creates enormous anxiety when I go to the doctor and the first place they point me is the bathroom. Oh no, not the cup. Anything but the cup! Why are they so small? It's not a precise activity for us females so how about a bowl? Men have it much easier; even with shaky hands I can't imagine it has a high degree of difficulty. All they have to do is stay awake and aim.

I found myself taking the dreaded walk to the bathroom at my internist's office. You'd think that after years of experience at the Ob-Gyn, I would have some level of skill and accuracy. My gynecologist's nurse says "there's the cup, pee and leave it on the shelf." Now I was staring at a step-by-step list of what to do that was taped on the wall. I'm not good at following rules and felt panicked; my hands started to shake.

There was a lovely basket of tiny cups with little blue lids, a nice Martha Stewart touch. I couldn't help but wonder if her aim is better than mine is. There was also a bowl of packaged towelettes for pre-peeing purposes. I couldn't get one of the tightly sealed packets opened. I grew anxious and looked around for the Xanax basket. When I finally tore it open with my teeth, the towel dropped on the floor. My first instinct was to just pick it up and continue. Is there a 15-second rule for towelettes? I opened another one. In my rush to be done, I dropped the cup I was holding. My first instinct was just to pick it up.

Profusely sweating and slightly dizzy, but with a new cup in hand, I was ready. I always think I'm in the general area but it's really hit or miss. Miss really sucks. It is a sad, pitiful, embarrassing moment and thankfully, I'm alone. I pray I'm not the only one who has this problem and yet in those moments believe I am. Yesterday I was lucky, first time on target. I did have to write my name on the label twice as my nerves were jangled and I couldn't remember how to spell "Gail."

Finally and triumphantly, I placed the cup on the shelf. Now I can relax until my next checkup. I wonder however, if I should practice before my next appointment.

Jewish Princess Blues

WHY DIDN'T I TAKE AUTO MECHANICS IN HIGH SCHOOL? I just watched a friend put a new engine in his truck. It was un-freaking believable! I was awestruck. Tools, wires, cables, nuts, bolts and screws were everywhere and he knew exactly what to do.

As a teenager, I was consumed with "what will I wear today" and couldn't be distracted by transmissions or carburetors. I indulged in the labor-intensive task of searching my closet for another new fashion combo. "Nope, wore that one three days ago," or "Mom, why isn't my blue print blouse ironed yet?" I whined mercilessly when I said it, and arrived at college unable to iron. I couldn't do anything except match clothes. Learning how to change a tire or the oil would have been far more educational and cheaper in the long run.

"Handy" people are a veritable religious experience to me. I'm dumbstruck by a person on a ladder with a tool in their hand. I want a tool also but ixnay the ladder. I'm afraid of heights. Am I hopeless or is it genetic? Perhaps I'm not predisposed to rewire a lamp or fix a faucet. My indestructible and tenacious Jewish Princess genes must have gone on a search and destroy mission for all my "handy" chromosomes. I have triumphantly mastered jiggling the handle of a running toilet. But hang on, I can also take off the top of the tank and look in. I don't know what to do next but it feels like an accomplishment. Eventually the irrefutable princess genes prevail and I call a repairman. I'm cursed, and saddened by his bill.

I stare longingly at my friend's tools and wonder what they do. I pick up a wrench and feel the urge to fix something. The urge passes.

Now, what should I wear?

Ninety-Five Year Old Man Looking for a Hookup

I'VE COME TO THE CONCLUSION THAT MEN believe they are never too old to pick up women. This is unfortunate because at some point it's creepy. I think there should be a cut-off age but sadly, there isn't.

I witnessed an ancient man hitting on women in a bar in Palm Desert on a Friday night. The average age out there is 65 but he hadn't seen that number in decades. There he sat, wearing a straw hat, dark aviator sunglasses, white crew neck sweater, and black collared shirt—looking exactly like Truman Capote. Nuzzled very close to him on his right was a plasticized 50ish buxom blonde in a tight, short, low cut white dress and push up bra. He looked like the cat that swallowed the canary or a boatload of Viagra.

I was staring and he was grinning. I tried to avert my eyes but couldn't. Inquisitive and incredulous, I asked the waitress his age.

"Oh he's 95. He's here all the time."

I didn't know whether to applaud his temerity or order a shot of Pepto-Bismol for my ensuing nausea. I could only conclude he must be the richest man west of the Mississippi. I turned away to take a sip of my martini and when I looked back he had a new woman sitting on his left. In the blink of an eye, another buxom blonde had materialized. My faux Truman Capote was double dipping.

I pestered the waitress for more information. "Who's the new woman and what's up with the first blonde?"

She spilled the beans. "The one on his right is just his friend. He had me give his card to the other woman so she would join him."

The card must read, "I'm over 90, have a heart condition and a billion dollars" because she had toddled over and plopped down next to him. Oh no, please stop; he was kissing her ear and nibbling on her neck. Again, I couldn't look away and prayed he had just fallen asleep. It seemed so wrong—like catching your parents having sex when you were little. I needed medication and blinders.

Uh oh and oh no, the ancient guy was looking in my direction. I think he crooked his finger for me to come over. I grabbed the edge of the bar so I didn't faint. I must admit he was a nervy critter. I can't imagine hanging out in a bar at 95, cruising for young hotties who at that age would be 75-year olds. I think I'd rather be home watching "Sex and the City" reruns and fantasizing about wearing high heels without falling.

Sex or the Internet?

SEX OR THE INTERNET? Hmm, which one would you give up for two weeks? This was a question posed in a survey I read. I, for one, have become an internet hermit, having given up the out of doors and social interaction to sit endlessly staring at my computer screen, which is a deeply disturbing thought. I don't have a beard the last I looked, but I need to recheck. No beard, but I could use a haircut. What season is it? Are short skirts in or out? Most importantly how much is gas? If I pick sex, I had better shower.

    I used to have a life. There was a time when I got up in the morning and got dressed but now my little laptop calls to me from my office. "Gail, I'm in here...come in...take a seat...you've got mail." Ah, mail. Is this the 21st century orgasm? I don't have to leave the tiny tantalizing little machine when I can get everything from refrigerators to tires to vibrators online. I can even shop for dates and never actually have to go on one, which is a real time saver. I love men I never have to meet—it's so much easier to get along.

How did this happen to me? I was a free spirited hippie, a flower child, a vegetarian and totally anti-establishment. Now I'm in my green robe from Target, hooked on technology. I can google every single ache and pain in my body. It's like a dream come true. I've spent hours just on my left knee. A diagnosis eludes me, but I'm getting close. And my cracking right thumb is still an enigma.

Is this turning you on, too? Are my medical symptoms better than foreplay? Are the words "you've got mail" hotter than that man or woman in your life? Is "Facebook" orgasmic? I bet you could tweet and have sex simultaneously but that's cheating. It's crunch time: No sex or no internet for two weeks. Could I google the answer?

Don't Call Me, I'll Call You

GOT SLYDIAL? IT SOUNDS TOO GOOD TO BE TRUE. No more nasty, bitter breakup talks, or that necessary but dreaded conversation with the ex about a late alimony payment. Slydial means never having someone on the other end of the phone again. It's almost poetry. There's no risk of a real person in real time answering. You get zapped directly to voice mail and voila, you leave a message. To think I could have saved my vocal cords and sanity during my divorce brings tears to my eyes. To say nothing of the phones I broke throwing them against the wall. No, I did not need an anger management class, just a new phone.

Slydial isn't cold and impersonal, it's freeing and verbally liberating. No matter how well I'd planned a break-up speech the other person always messed it up by expressing their feelings. Having to interrupt with, "I'm not a selfish bitch who hates your mother" made me forget what else I was going to say. Speaking of mothers, slydial will eliminate her endless line of questioning. I may get a job just because it would be so easy to call in sick.

Slydial is so much better than text messages. Watching all those crazy texters with their thumbs and fingers flying a mile a minute across the tiny keys makes me dizzy. Besides, wacky word abbreviations are mind numbing as are the confusing emojis replacing syntax. So rest assured, I will not send some impersonal breakup text message any time soon. It will be a cowardly voice mail.

Who Are the People in *People*?

IT IS SHOCKING AND DEEPLY DISTURBING to admit that I no longer know anyone in *People Magazine*. I actually used to look forward to reading it in line at the grocery store. What better and cheaper way to pass the time behind someone whose cart is piled to overflowing than grabbing the *People* and finishing it before it's your turn? It was so entertaining that I didn't even start screaming and crying when folks pulled out coupons that took 30 minutes for the checkout girl to decipher. I loved a crowded grocery store.

I also actually looked forward to the dentist as, God love him, he keeps his subscription to *People* current. I have spent many happy hours in his waiting room catching up on back issues. I even read them between Novocaine shots. *People* magazine was a secret vice; I never confessed that I read it. I've even put it inside *The New Yorker* to protect my image. Don't ask what "image"—it just makes me feel better to think I have one to uphold.

Now I open the precious magazine and turn page after page after page and think to myself, "who are these people?" I have no idea. Apparently, they are famous but I have to ask where, why and how? It scares me that they are in movies and videos I've never heard of or seen. The Announcement page makes me lunge for medication when the people in the birthday paragraph are half my age. I could be everyone's mother or worse, nana! Again, I ask myself, who are these people and why don't I know them? Where are the stars I used to love? Faye Dunaway, come back I need you. Make a movie or music video with Harrison Ford so I can sleep at night.

I won't even start on the music videos I have never seen, by artists whose names are just two letters, both being consonants. Thankfully, I know Lady GaGa but might have just capitalized it incorrectly. I bet she's happy her mom made her take piano lessons. I also hope Justin Bieber reaches puberty soon or he should seek medical attention. Mick Jagger come back to me but please stop having children with women younger than your other children.

Sadly, I now stand in the grocery store line or sit in my dentist's office tempted to pick up the *People* but knowing it will only serve to remind me that the pages are filled with stars who could call me nana.

II.
Really!

"Mirror, Mirror on the Wall, That Can't Be Me"

BY MISTAKE, I GLANCED IN THE HALL MIRROR on my way downstairs. I think I briefly lost consciousness before letting out a small shriek. I surprised me. Whoa, who was that? I backed up and took a closer look. I needed emergency lipstick, eyeliner and rouge or it actually wasn't me but my mother. I quickly decided to try another mirror and ran to the bathroom. Cannily, and to save myself from personal ruin at 10:15 a.m., I only turned on one of the three light switches. So much better, although I was squinting. Squinting definitely improved my skin tone and I decided not to call my therapist. Truthfully, it is a shock to "catch" myself in the mirror these days. When did the prom girl version disappear?

I was whining to my girlfriend Betsy about my mirror experience.

"Oh honey, just do what I do, look at one very small part of your face at a time."

I still wasn't comforted. "Do men our age feel this way? Do they ever think they look like crap?"

"Lord no, they have "magic" mirrors. No matter how old, gray, bald and wrinkled they are, they don't see it."

"I want a magic mirror too," I sobbed.

"Sorry sweetie we don't get to have them. I gotta run, but like I said, one tiny part at a time."

She was right; men have "magic" mirrors. I met a short, fat, balding 65-year old in an oversized Nike t-shirt and jeans that skimmed the top of his ankles who spent an evening telling me he only liked to date women in their fifties. Has he looked in the mirror lately? Or the guy next to me at the bar at Sullivan's with a smile on his face and a comb over. He definitely has a magic mirror and should never go out on a windy day or swim. I can't forget 64-year old Alan, a never been married retired lawyer with a hairpiece dyed burnt umber, who proceeded to declare he always has sex with a woman by the third date or "good-bye." He must never look in the mirror, and should definitely get a new colorist as well as therapist.

I envy these men with their magic mirrors…or is it cataracts?

"Bathrobe Woman" vs. My Bank Account

I CAN'T GET OUT OF MY BATHROBE. I need help. I put on clothes to go out for food and wine but the minute I get home, I rip them off and on goes my comfy green robe. Not an attractive look. I've tried to dress it up with my black suede Kate Spade high heels, but it's definitely a fashion faux pas. Yet, as bad I look, I can't take it off. I've become (drum roll) "Bathrobe Woman!"

Step aside Spider Man. Courageously wrapped in my robe, I have dragged myself down the driveway for the newspaper and even walked the dog in my greenness. Weather is no obstacle—rain, snow, sleet or hail, I'm going. I haven't been arrested for unnecessary and indecent exposure yet but a Jack Russell Terrier stopped chasing a squirrel to bark at me. "Shoo little critter and don't jump on the outfit." A neighbor reminded me I wasn't dressed; duh, I think I'm aware of that. Leave me alone, I'm in my financial panic protection gear.

Being "Bathrobe Woman" keeps me safe from monetary ruin. It prevents me from going out and purchasing the two pairs of shoes I have on hold at Neiman Marcus. It keeps me away from the cosmetic counter at Saks and Lord knows I could desperately use makeup. I stay home curled up with the L.L. Bean catalogue and any desire to buy new clothes vanishes. Just say a big fat "no" to khaki pants, topsiders, and fleece sheets. I sit in front of the TV watching reruns of *Friends* and *Grey's Anatomy* wrapped in my cozy green cocoon. I'm cranky that there are no new shows that I like, but happy I haven't spent the $6.00 in my wallet and my credit card is safely frozen in a block of ice.

As "Bathrobe Woman" I've found a way to beat my bank account blues yet long for the day I can shed my protective outfit, thaw out my Visa card and hightail it back to Neimans for those shoes.

Dad, Poor Dad, I've Caught Him Watching Porn and I'm Feeling So Sad

DO YOU WATCH PORN? I DON'T. Does your dad? Mine does. And, is there psychological well-being after catching your dad in the act of watching?

I read that porn is the largest industry on the internet, which surprised me for some reason. Was I thinking it was really Oprah? Sorry babe, the people like porn better. It appears millions of men and women are logging on at all hours of the day and night. Is there an appropriate snack food?

I dated a man who sat bleary-eyed in front of his computer screen, checking out the free sites. He was too cheap to pay, so who needed him. Would you call this a hobby? Would you list it on a resume under "outside activities"? My dad's retired, so thankfully he doesn't have the resume dilemma.

I never knock when I visit my parents. Everyone in the family has a key, so per usual I walked in unannounced, dog in tow, at about 3:00 p.m. There's Dad in his giant lounge chair watching TV, and straight ahead on the screen was a porno movie. My dad was 87. What happened to Little Joe on *Bonanza*? Where's *The Sound of Music*? There's not a Von Trapp Family singer in sight, just a blowjob.

Holy crap! I was torn between bursting into laughter or running out of the room screaming while throwing back Valium and ripping out my pocket Freud. He saw me and jumped up as fast as he could, although not fast enough, and fumbled with the clicker to get it off the screen. This took a lifetime. I looked down, and mumbled something about taking the dog out on the deck for air. It was I who needed the oxygen.

What does a daughter do next? Stay? Go? Ask him who his favorite porn star is? Call a caregiver for myself? "Oh my God, oh my God," was all I could choke out as I paced the deck. Why me? Why not my sister? Why did she get special dispensation? I'm older; I have less time to live joyfully. I had to call her and ruin her life too. Denial was my only move, and coincidentally it was my dad's. He appeared on the deck with the same resolve. What movie? We made our usual "weather" small talk and then I fled.

I couldn't dial my sister fast enough. "Answer already!" I was screaming and pounding the phone on the dashboard like that would help her pick up. I got her machine. Damn. I couldn't be alone with this information; I had to tell someone, or everyone. I thought seriously about confiding in the guy behind the counter at the 7-11 when I stopped for a soda. Could he double as a counselor or exorcist? And why the hell wasn't my sister returning my call?

I ixnayed the clerk and called my friend Don. I made his day. He laughed nonstop for ten minutes. I finally joined in and tears were streaming down my face, I was laughing or crying so hard. Then he abruptly stopped and proclaimed, "I'll pay for the first three hours of analysis."

In the aftermath of my trauma, I discovered that my tale of Freudian horror made a great story. Everyone loved it. Dad was cheered on by my friends. He had become a geriatric hero, with icon status in his demographic. I'm shocked, and they're awed. Hey, what if it was your dad?

I Confess: I Am Not "Hip" Anymore

AFTER 200 HOURS OF WATCHING coverage of Donald Trump's first 100 days, I decided I needed a break from talks of impeachment and collusion, and from Anderson Cooper. I am a little disappointed he has abandoned his signature yellow rain slicker for suits and skinny ties. I am jealous of his cheekbones, though. Regardless, I decided to finally pick up the clicker and do a little channel surfing. I needed to seek refuge from the political maelstrom and hightailed it to a "Miami Crime Scene" and brutal "Cupcake War." This proved to be very bad thinking.

On my travels up the channels, I made an ill-fated stop at the MTV Music Video Awards and there it suddenly struck me; I had no idea who anyone was. Not one familiar face. Why didn't I just keep going? Where's Elton John when you need him? Lady Gaga—who I usually recognize by her life-threateningly tall high heels—was dressed like a man. Did she do this to screw with me? For God's sake, help me out and put on the giant shoes.

I think I've become a loser. It was a night of reckoning. Did this happen in the blink of an eye? One day the audience is filled with the likes of The Grateful Dead, Neil Young, Bob Dylan, Eric Clapton et al. and then—POOF—they're gone, replaced by a group of pink-haired girls and boys covered in ink. Where have I been? I should have known this day was coming, as the people in *People Magazine* are total strangers to me now as well. They look so young that any one of them could conceivably call me "Nana." This is very stressful. I need George Clooney to be the hottest man alive again, not married with children.

I have to face it and confess; I am not "hip" anymore. I have tried to keep up. I wear short skirts, have long hair and still love to "hang out" but it's obviously not enough. Sadly, it's possible I haven't been hip since 1974 when I went to a party at Jerry Garcia's ranch. My hip-o-meter has plunged to zero.

"Lady Gaga, please put on a dress and 9-inch heels again so I can recognize one person but don't ever call me Nana."

I Hate *The New Yorker*

I HAVE A SECRET. IT'S TOO SHAMEFUL TO ADMIT. I can hardly spit it out but maybe it will be purging. I'll try; bear with me. I dread getting *The New Yorker*. Oh Lord, I've said it. Be merciful.

Getting a subscription was a huge mistake, like my second divorce attorney. The subscription seemed like a good idea at the time. My mother was taking a course on the magazine and my son was an avid reader. I felt stupid when they talked about articles and I had no knowledge of the subjects. I had to have in.

Now when I see yet another one in my mailbox my stomach sinks, my blood pressure rises and I get a rash. "Crap, not *The New Yorker* again," I cry out. The mailman thinks I'm nuts. Didn't they just send one? Why isn't this freaking subscription up already? I'm tempted to throw it away, but stop myself and instead make a solemn vow I'll read it. Yes, more than just the cartoons.

The articles are too long. And can anyone really see the print? It's a lethal combination for someone in a hurry and with the attention span of a nearsighted gnat. I always take a cursory look, a yes or no as to what I want to read. Admittedly, and this is a tough admission, I ixnay most of the magazine. It just doesn't seem that interesting. There I confess: "IT DOESN'T SEEM THAT INTERESTING."

Right now, I have one New Yorker by my bed, one in my car and one on the floor of the bathroom. They're like roaches.

Have I become an idiot? I had so much intellectual promise, too. Wait a minute, hold on a second. For the record, I did read a very long article on the artist John Currin. I also entered the cartoon caption contest twice. I thought I'd win; I lost.

I've done this before. I subscribed to *The New York Review of Books*. Each week I excitedly looked through the newest arrival and then put it in a drawer next to my bed for leisure reading. Fifty-two weeks later, I had a fire hazard. It was a day of intellectual reckoning when I threw them all away. I did it without therapy but did develop hives and small fever. I'm looking forward to the week my subscription to *The New Yorker* ends. I may throw a party—cash bar, no food. I do have promise after all.

I'm Calling a Cab

TO HIKE OR NOT TO HIKE? "Not" is the right answer. And it isn't good to learn the hard way after the age of 50.

My sister, who apparently has mountain goat genes, invited me on what was billed as an easy eight-mile hike with her club in Palm Springs. I was on vacation and up for something new. It sounded like good exercise and we could spend some quality time chitchatting along the way.

She woke me up at 6:00 a.m. to get ready. I hate 6:00 a.m. She was busy in the kitchen packing food and water into our backpacks when I dragged my sorry ass over to the coffee pot. I hate backpacks; the last time I wore one I cried. I had to go back to bed. I needed more rest to carry everything. Oh God, what if I had to pee? "You squat behind a rock," my sister calmly advised me. Were those tears in my eyes? I suddenly itched all over.

Richard, our hike leader was an ex-Navy navigator who handed each of us a map complete with land elevations and route. He was prepared and I was confused. I can't read a map. I was a loser as a Brownie and did not get one Girl Scout badge. He made us yell a head count, which was either the closet kindergarten teacher in him, or a sign he could lose one of us. I vowed to stick to him like Gorilla Glue.

As we headed into Joshua Tree National Park at 9:30 a.m., I looked back longingly at the bathroom near the entrance. Every time we stopped to check the map, I said the same thing, "Do you know where we are? Are we lost?" Richard glared at me but I wouldn't be deterred. "Are you SURE you know where we are?"

How can I explain what happened next? One of the men was attacked by a cactus; a jumping Cholla got him on the calf. Since when did plants jump? Enemy combatant plants were out there and no one told me. I almost fainted as I watched the clump of needles be removed from his leg with a comb. Richard said the needles could go through your hiking boots into the bones of your feet. (Had I known about the killer cactus...) I needed Valium. No, what I really needed was a TAXI!

We trudged on through the sand until the path led us into a canyon with only one way out, and that was straight up. Did I mention the trail disappeared, replaced by giant boulders? My sister referred to this part of the day as "boulder scrambling." I preferred to call it, "I hate hiking." I was getting very testy and wanted to go home, but as Richard explained, the "beauty" of hiking is you have to finish. I hated him also. I crawled up and over boulders with the help of the man behind me who I begged to put both hands on my butt and push me. After 2 1/2 miles, the day-before manicure was shot as was my anterior cruciate ligament.

I almost burst into tears when I saw the car on the horizon. I loved the car. I was hot, sweaty, beet red, and practically toxic from not peeing. Five hours and 8.2 miles later I was not a better person nor a hiker. And, btw, my sister and I never did chitchat.

Next time I take a hike, I'm taking it in a cab.

Mid-Fork a Tarnished Romance

I HAVE NO IDEA HOW TO SET A TABLE. Is the spoon the loner or paired with a fork? What about the knife? In a moment of table setting panic, I feel like turning it on myself. Oh my God, what if there are two forks, then what—inside of the spoon, outside the knife? I'm dizzy and confused. Uh oh, the napkin—who gets that? The urge to sob into it seems like the proper use. I'm getting a rash and holding inexplicable silverware. I usually give up and throw myself on the mercy of the nearest human because EVERYONE but me knows how to set a table. I've been instructed on numerous occasions and just heard "blah, blah, blah." Going out to dinner is so much easier and doesn't require another reading of *When Bad Things Happen to Good People.*

I wasn't prepared for a fork to seek revenge or become an enemy agent. Confused? So was I. The surprise attack came on a vacation with my new boyfriend. It started off with a really GOOD surprise—a romantic mid-winter getaway to

La Jolla. Adios down parka, down vest, neck warmer, scarf, hat, Timberland boots that weigh more than I do and potholder-style mittens. The Michelin Man look would soon be replaced by skimpy cotton clothes—like a dream come true for this winter hater. The boyfriend even took me out shopping for lingerie, which seemed like a harbinger of desire.

The airplane ride was uneventful, no reason to be anything but happy the Southern California coast was in my future. I had brought enough clothing for a trip lasting a year, not five days, but "be prepared" was my fashion motto and I pictured many outfit changes for all our fun-filled activities. We were staying at The Lodge at Torre Pines where one look at the green, green golf course made me long to be a golfer; could I learn by dinner?

With no time to unpack before our restaurant reservations, I put on the outfit closest to the top of the giant pile in my suitcase, grabbed a pair of sexy high heels and headed down to the dining room. Nothing unusual to report during the salad or first glass of wine, just idle chitchat about the lovely weather. The silverware seemed to be perfectly placed so I tried to take a mental picture for future reference (ha ha).

Being someone who flunks idle chatter, I changed the subject to something peripherally political. I swear there was no mention of the name Trump. We were in what I thought was the Trump Free Zone. I do, however, remember using the words "weaponizing religion." Now isn't that an interesting subject? I thought so. Not when your partner thinks weapons aren't metaphors but real guns best used in a military context. Bang!

Can you say "conversational free fall?" There was no analogy, metaphor, parable, simile or part of speech that could change the course of events. "I think you're taking this too seriously" did not work. I could see the expression on his face morph into Darth Vader, and his breathing became metallic. I was not going over to the dark side so I gulped the remaining wine and glanced down at my salmon. When I looked up, he was coming at me with a fork loaded with medium rare lamb chop. Mid-way across the table it came to a halt and he blurted out "This isn't going to work." Huh? Was I officially on the shortest romantic getaway in history—less than 45 minutes? I had no response other than to ask if the lamb chop was good.

I got up, stared at the fork still hovered over the table, vowed to never learn its correct placement, and took the next train to LA.

Studying the Tribal Women of Orange County

JUST WHEN I THOUGHT THE WORLD couldn't possibly get any scarier, it did. I watched *The Housewives of Orange County*. Why, would I do this when I was terrified by the *Twilight Zone* and *Shock Theater* as a child? The Housewives are definitely *Shock Theater* revisited and make Freddy Kruger look like a fun, attractive guy to date. Who are these "Orange" housewives and how did they get a TV show?

It was eerily like watching the Travel Channel's *Living with the Mek* except, instead of traveling with two whacked out British boys studying this ancient Amazon tribe, I felt like Margaret Mead observing the lives of a back stabbing, foot stamping, narcissistic, garishly ornamented band of 40 year-old women living and procreating in Orange County, California.

Anthropologically speaking, their most notable and common feature was their GIANT breasts. I'm talkin' huge.

Parental discretion advised huge. I pondered whether this was a form of tribal status or the work of plastic surgeons on crack. I was miffed and a bit grossed out.

Their clothing was equally confusing. Perhaps the blindingly colored, short, low cut dresses were a way to frighten away predators in the wilds of Orange County, or a fashion tribute to Wilma Flintstone. Personally, I was scared and tempted to turn off the TV so as not to have really bad dreams.

Shamefully, I observed the "Orange Tribe" for three hours, which included the season finale. Unfortunately their breasts didn't explode, which would have been a really good cliffhanger. In the end, and anthropologically speaking, I kept asking myself the same questions: can these really be women, can lives be this empty, and is this crazed orange girl tribe on the endangered species list?

Don't Grow Old with Me

CRAP, IT'S TIME TO CHOOSE BETWEEN THE HAPPINESS derived from sugar and living to 120. That's a tough decision and not to be made lightly or when jacked up on a double mocha latte. If it's longevity you desire, "put the Snickers down and step away from the candy machine." Dr. Ahmet Oz, the medical guru, says there's a way to be old, older and the oldest one alive. The key, according to the Doc, is calorie restriction and, even worse, no sugar. Ixnay to the warm cuddly feeling a Twinkie provides. If you want something sweet, chew on a sweet potato or munch on kale. Yummy. Bring on the legumes and watch your 90's fly by.

Personally, I don't mind the fruits and vegetables required or the paltry 1,500 calories a day, as calorie counting is my math strength. I am also the only person who loses weight on a vacation to Italy; I'm no fun to travel with. I do however love Mounds bars and giving them up to become really old is not enticing.

But the bigger question for me is, why, why, why would I want to be 120? Correct me if I'm wrong but that doesn't sound like fun. I'd probably look like crap and regret not having my face lifted at 100. I doubt I could wear my fab high heels for fear of falling or my clingy little black strapless dress for fear of scaring people. And for everyone who thinks I complain a lot now, I think I would raise it to the level of a competitive sport. Clearly, I'd have no friends and multiple restraining orders issued against me.

Can you imagine what it would be like sitting around with fellow 120-year olds or those upstart kids in their late 90s? What would we talk about? Not sex, as the visuals would be way too disturbing. Prune juice with a Milk of Magnesia chaser is a favorite cocktail of my 100-year old Mother. No alcohol for fear of getting tipsy and actually tipping over. And would designer diaper bags be de rigueur?

Bring on the Twinkies.

Girls, Uncle Sam Wants You!

THE MARINES WANT ME! Hard to believe but hope springs eternal that someone does. I just read they are desperately seeking "a few good women." Coincidentally, I could stand a career change. I look good in blue, although I'd prefer black. Perhaps I could suggest a fashion update regarding color and uniform style. I should call the Secretary of Defense. Maybe Ralph Lauren or Stella McCartney could design something tasty. "Join the Marines and if you survive boot camp you get to keep the clothes." I like it and it's tempting.

It seems the Marines are specifically trying to appeal to female athletes, as they would be more likely to make it through boot camp with the men. Kind of like boy/girl after school sports, right? This really piques my interest. I loved beating the boys. I hope there's ice skating as I'd whip everyone's ass.

I'm a little concerned about the accommodations. I'm vehement about bedding and towels. For starters, I must have a queen-size bed so I can spread out and not feel cramped. I'm assuming I can bring my own pillows. I take them on all my sleepovers. I also insist on bath sheets, as I hate skimpy little towels after I shower. Whoops, I almost forgot, and this is big, I won't share a bathroom. Who can stand someone in your way at the sink, or all their stuff around when you put on makeup? Besides, it's my library and reading room. I need solitude.

I am, however, very excited about a communal dining experience. I love good conversation at meals. I hope there's a cocktail hour as it's such a nice way to relax and socialize at the end of a hectic day. I'm not a picky eater so you won't find me complaining about the food like some people. Just please no Mexican, Chinese, or Indian cuisine. For that matter, I never touch anything fried, or prepared in corn oil. I don't eat meat either.

Ok, admittedly no one wants me, not even the Marines. Could I still keep the clothes?

Bye-Bye Rio

OH NO, THE SUMMER OLYMPICS WERE OVER! Now what was to become of me, and my poor friend Dan who had three TVs going day and night? Sorry babe, no more 3:00 a.m. rowing or skeet shooting. It's official and final, I saw it with my own eyes; the Olympic torch has been extinguished.

Bye-bye, tiny Chinese girls. I'm guessing 12 was your real age, but I lie too. I would like to give every member of the American men's swim team my address and phone number. And I'm very sad I didn't spend more time watching men's beach volleyball, as the guys were super-hot.

I had one really big problem with these Olympics however. Can someone please tell me why the women's beach volleyball team had to play in bikinis? Was the late Hugh Hefner on the International Olympic Committee? They were wearing thongs, not sports uniforms. If it were me, I'd be standing there pulling the tiny pants out of my butt and lose track of the ball. Think of all that itchy nasty sand in all the wrong places. I'd also like to slap the person who picked white as the color those poor girls wore in the finals. Again, I can't help but wonder if that was Hef's idea. For God's sake, think of the body waxing it involved. I cringe at the thought, as I do not have that high a pain threshold. Those girls are resilient and hairless.

Sadly, it was time to find an Olympic free life. I hope that I can make the adjustment without therapy or medication. Hold on, I almost forgot, I didn't need a life. I had Democrats and Republicans to entertain me for the next two weeks at their respective conventions. I bet the competition would be fiercer than women's gymnastics. The X Games or World Wide Wrestling has nothing on political conventions. A veritable slugfest for "political gold"—the Presidency. I pray, however, that they are all wearing lots and lots of clothing.

"For Richer or for Richer"

HAS ANYONE CONSIDERED THE IMPACT a bad economy has on trophy wives? It must be really hard for them when the old guy's stock portfolio plummets. Stress causes wrinkles, girls, so be sure and have your plastic surgeon on speed dial. What is a person to do when "for richer or for poorer" becomes the dreaded "for poorer?" Not what you signed up for, is it? Don't fret; maybe old men are fun even without money. The two of you will have quality alone time now that charity galas are not in the budget. I know you loved the designer party clothes, but sweatpants are fun for staying home. Perk them up with some jewelry, if it's not being auctioned. There's love without Cartier, right? Listen up—buying nail polish at Walgreens is a real cash saver. Did I say something sad? With no money for open-toed Jimmy Choos or Manolos, think of the savings on pedicures. Frugality can be tons of fun.

About the second home, who needed all that packing and rescheduling of massages? I'm certain you didn't marry for a little old house in Aspen or St. Barts. You know what else "for poorer" means? No more personal trainer. So, sweetheart, step away from the brownies. I feel your pain because I love brownies also. I hope it isn't too late to renegotiate those crazy wedding vows. How does "for richer or for richer" sound now?

I'm curious. Are any of the trophy girls longing for their premarital boyfriends—the age appropriate hotties that had hair, height, no body fat and didn't need a Viagra prescription? It's funny what can happen even after you say, "I do" in a $50,000 Vera Wang wedding dress.

Relationship "Deal Breakers" or Living Alone

LET'S FACE IT; WE ALL HAVE RELATIONSHIP DEAL BREAKERS, either in the form of a laundry list or in one little idiosyncratic thing about another person that drives us crazy. I know it's hard to confess but let's be honest—it's true. Sadly, I probably have more deal breakers than years left.

My buddy Gary recently told me how he narrows down his prospective mates. Smokers are out, even those trying to quit. Ixnay to anyone bearing cigarettes, nicotine patches, or anything that emits smoke. I'm with Gary on this one, but he lost me on the toilet paper and paper towel criteria. Whoa G, that's tough for some poor unsuspecting date just trying to help out around the house. Does she put the paper on the roll so it comes off the top or bottom? I've never given that a thought. Top is the correct answer to the toilet paper quiz to remain in Gary's heart. Interesting, but chances are he'll end up alone. Personally, I like the paper to come from the bottom but my list is too long already. And as for which way shirts face on the hangers, I suggest Gary seek counseling immediately.

I confess I'm a laundry-list dater. Bad shoes are a big no-no in my book. My shoe scrutinizing eyes go right to some poor guy's feet. I'm from the loafer or topsider days and I'm stickin' to it. Absolutely no sandals, that's the worst. I don't care if it's 120 degrees outside—men over 30 must wear close-toed shoes. Old men feet make me want to run for cover. And never ever think that wearing socks with sandals helps.

I feel bad if a man has male pattern baldness but my sympathy doesn't extend to dating. Do not cover it up with a hairpiece or scary looking plugs; cut it very short or take it all off. What happens if I don't see you without fake hair until the first night we have sex and off it comes and I have a heart attack? One more little hint: do not color your hair. Men never have good colorists and end up looking like my least favorite shade in the Crayola box, "Burnt Umber."

Moving on, if you own anything that ticks, destroy it. Have an overhead fan that whirs too loudly and incessantly, you're out. One snore, no matter how faint, and we say goodbye at 3:00 a.m. Shhh. And I'm tired of talking about politics especially if we don't agree; blah, blah, blah, no opinions welcome until the next election cycle.

I don't go on many dates and have sought counseling.

Baby Boomers, Be Afraid, Be Very Afraid...and Don't Watch TV

FELLOW BABY BOOMERS BE AFRAID, be very afraid. Madison Avenue is after us and they're getting too close for comfort. I'm trying as hard as I can to be strong and stay away from the TV, even though my big flat screen is a good way to see someone's pores and feel better about my own. Admittedly however, I'm weak, with little willpower when it comes to "regularly scheduled programming" as opposed to BREAKING NEWS which scares the shit out of me.

Sunday morning I tried as hard as humanly possible to turn my back on George Stephanopoulos and his giant hair. I walked through my den head down, putting one foot carefully in front of the other. Coffee was the only thing on my mind.

"I love coffee, I can't wait for my morning coffee, I love coffee, I can't wait."

Who was I kidding; I grabbed the seven clickers it takes to turn on the TV. Crap, which stupid piece of plastic gets me a station? I had all seven in my hand ready to throw at the wall when it occurred to me that would be counter-productive. I had a slight fever and mild delirium when George's face and hair finally appeared.

If only the morning was filled with my usual yelling and swearing at the screen but alas, it wasn't. The commercials freaked me out. They may as well have called my name. "Gail, are you irritable and bloated because you're constipated?" No, well sometimes, maybe, should I be? "Gail, are you sleepless? Do you toss and turn and rip the covers to shreds?" Ok, yes, yes, a thousand times yes! What do I need, tell me, tell me. "Gail, would you like to flatten your flabby abs?" Oh God, they can see my abs. I sucked in my stomach and spit out my coffee. "Gail, are you having trouble reading the menu and sorry you went out to dinner?" Ah ha, at last I got them! "I can read the menu." No, I lied; I can't read the menu. I just pretend and order fish.

I no longer cared about George, his big hair or his political opinions. I hated him and his cruel advertisers. I vowed to go out to dinner because I might be constipated, exhausted and flabby but I could order fish!

Help! My House is Surrounded by the Starbucks Police!

I'M A HERETIC. I DID SOMETHING UNHEARD OF, veritably blasphemous. I don't think there were any witnesses, although I can't be certain. I had to do it. Regardless of whether or not the economy is getting stronger, I'm not. I'm still cheap, and unable to resist a bargain no matter how irreverent.

I was in need of coffee and because the little brown beans have taken on religious significance as well as social status, I always reach for a pound of Starbucks or Peets. The blends continue to confuse me but I usually pick a country I'd like to visit like Italy, France or Kenya and remind myself that buying the mind-bending expensive roast is cheaper than a plane ticket, but not much. So there I was ready to break the bank for beans when I see a much cheaper option. A brand I've never heard of at $5.99 for 12 ounces—be still my heart.

Does anyone else think coffee drinks have taken over our minds, sanity and wallets? What ever happened to Maxwell House and "good to the last drop?" Mom used to make it every morning and I loved the very blue can. Who can forget Mrs. Folger regardless of her bad hairdo and pathetic taste in clothes? Personally I loved Chock Full of Nuts, or was I nuts?

Now it's every man for themselves in the line at Starbucks. I've witnessed the madness and yes, paid $7.00 for an espresso. I don't even understand what anyone's ordering. Are they speaking a romance language or Latin? All that comes to my mind is "huh?" Ironically, no one is even happy about their order. They're angrily pushing and shoving me aside or sending back a "grande" because they ordered a "vente." I'm thinking they're over-caffeinated before the caffeine. "Excuse me but the Valium line is to the right."

I'm also wondering whether nonfat whipped cream is an oxymoron. Have the real stuff for God's sake; it's all fattening. I love the order of "grande, but a little less than grande, with latte but not too latte, half steamed, half air, half nonfat, half mocha and that's to go."

Personally, I think it's all the same drink. I stare at the cheap little bag of beans and realize I'm not actually ready or determined enough to buy them. I decide to have a coke.

Labor Day or Laborious Day?

NO, NOT ANOTHER HOLIDAY WEEKEND! These are a special kind of torture for me. I can't stand the pressure to use the grill and invite people over which requires cleaning and appetizers. This sounds less and less like a celebration with every added chore. A holiday really should be where you sit around alone in a messy house, read back issues of *People*, eat potato chips out of the bag and drink wine from a plastic cup—no cheeriness required. This also eliminates the risk of ptomaine or salmonella from nasty yet traditional holiday foods like eight-hour old coleslaw, undercooked chicken, or the dreaded hot dog on a stick. What's in a hot dog anyway and why a stick?

Is there a parade on Labor Day—I can't remember. Do I need to dress up the dog like a Disney character and hope she doesn't bite a small child? And being unemployed, do I march in the parade or just stand on the side waving a tiny flag? I'm not a parade person, employed or otherwise. I do like the one that has a giant inflated Mickey Mouse, however.

The long holiday weekend looms ahead. I feel the tension rising and my arms getting itchy. I should lock the door, pull down the shades, break out the back issues of *People* and hope I have enough chips and wine to make it to Tuesday.

No labor required.

I Hate Packing Boxes!

LET'S FACE IT, MOVING SUCKS. It forces me to take a good hard look at all the crap I've acquired and dragged from place to place because I refuse to admit it's crap. Why do I still have madras Bermuda shorts in my closet and a mink coat with one arm? If anyone wants either item, please let me know ASAP. I'm a little afraid to move the coat, however, for fear of it becoming a vest. I have shoes that are too small, which make me wonder if they ever fit, and if they didn't, why I bought them. I have a small red purse and hate red. I have two white blouses that haven't been white since 1998 and my friend Ellen's University of Wisconsin sweatshirt that I forgot to return in 1973.

I've become an expert at packing up a kitchen. I'm fast, good and have a low breakage record. My biggest weakness is the tape gun—not a pretty sight. I've yet to master wielding the tape and holding the bottom of the carton closed. I scream a lot and have on occasion thrown the box down and stomped on it. Crying doesn't help. And just say no to taping and drinking, but if you must, be sure and have plenty of gauze and Band-Aids. Stacking up boxes filled with pots and pans I rarely use, and the expensive china that has never seen a meal, makes me ponder why I even need a kitchen. I don't have the time or enough medication to explore that right now.

Once I start, I'm a packing machine. Tape gun in hand, like a Special Ops soldier I invade my office. Without warning, I throw away a *Village Voice* from 1972. I have no idea why I saved it—which scares me—but I trash it anyway. Pictures, books, #2 pencils, my old Filofax, all go in boxes. A single coaster is tossed, although I do drink alone so I pause to reconsider. Pictures of me with short hair nearly cause me to faint, but I'm on a mission. Horrified, I vow never to consider cutting it again. I'm sweaty but satisfied my life is piled up in corrugated boxes. I make a solemn vow not to move again until I eat at least one meal on the china.

Home Alone

MEN SHOULD NEVER RETIRE. It's scary to consider your guy home all day. I don't care how long you've been together, it doesn't sound like fun. If you're an anthropologist, it might be interesting because a strange thing happens to men when they stop working; they become women. They're not very good at it, however. Being a woman at home requires multi-tasking at the highest level; no loitering, ruminating or lounging allowed. It's go, go, go from the moment you wake up.

Turn the house over to your man and step aside because nothing is about to get done. Oh, maybe one thing, as a man going to the cleaners takes a significant part of the day. Then there's grocery shopping, which is draining. Of course, because your boy didn't make a list he has to go back for the item he went for originally. He did, however, buy four boxes of frozen blueberry waffles that no one will ever eat. Why don't men believe in lists? It must be like asking for directions. You're a housewife now, write things down.

Am I being mean? After all, job transitions are difficult. Going from CEO to putting laundry away could take time, so in the adjustment period just pile the clothes on the bed as there's no rush to put them away. About the vacuum that I just tripped and fell over? Don't worry, I'm fine and you're right, don't put it back. It looks nice in the bathroom. Did I mention how creative I think it is to use the ironing board as a place to pile the bills and tools?

Maybe men should never be allowed to retire. Although on second thought, they deserve to be the wife they thought had nothing to do all day. The woman they were certain just sat around. I think they are in for a very big surprise.

So anthropologists take note as the business man evolves into the business of being a woman.

Blue M&Ms

MOTHER NATURE MUST BE A MAN. Women get menopause and men get Viagra. Is this a midlife sleight of hand or a dirty trick? The pharmaceutical industry is complicit in this also, as the little pills are doing landmark business. And let's not forget the doctors who are handing these babies out like they are blue M&Ms. The world of relationships is now on tilt.

Women do not lose their sex drive on purpose. It's menopause, not personal. Men should not get pissed off and pout that their wife, significant other or girlfriend is denying them sex to be mean. I've seen plenty of middle-aged men who should be denied food to get rid of that beach ball they swallowed. And wasn't the midlife crisis Porsche enough happiness?

Women aren't focused on sex and it's no fault of their own; their hormones are gone, vanished, hasta la bye-bye. Big Pharma, how about making hormone replacement drugs for us that are safe? I personally would like my dewy complexion back. (Did you think I'd say sex drive?)

My friend Jack tried to help. He called to tell me about an article he read regarding a libido-enhancing drug they're working on for older women. Isn't it possible women are happy with their lives? So what, if we're not fantasizing about sex. Personally, I've noticed there are not too many fantasy men in my demographic.

Ironically, my male friends have no interest in having sex with an older woman or even one their own age. They must not have mirrors. Should we cry, call a plastic surgeon or seek counseling? I suggest sex with a younger man. That sounds like hormone replacement therapy to me.

"Princess Stripped of Crown!" or I Hate to Shop

I HATE CLOTHES SHOPPING. Shopping is at the top of my 'most dreaded' list. This is no more evident than looking in my closet, where my friend Adria recently spent about 30 seconds before she started screaming. "Is this it? Where are the rest of your clothes?"

Sheepishly I stammered, "I don't know...oh wait...there are a few things in my office closet." I took her hand, marched her in there and stood with my head down so as not to witness her expression.

"Are you kidding? There's no such thing as a Jewish princess with so little clothing!"

Crap, I was busted and demoted. I felt ashamed and questioned the validity of my DNA. She was right; I was a disgrace to my "title" and to my mother, who could dress the entire third world with the clothes in her closet that she has never even worn.

I was determined to prove Adria wrong. I *was* a Jewish Princess! With trepidation and medication, I set forth. First stop, J. Crew, where I had my friend Karen on speakerphone.

"Now go to the back of the store and look at the minis; they are so cute," she commanded. "Then you definitely need the little blue pinstriped jacket with the rolled up cuffs. Oh, and ask the salesman to show you the jeans in all those great colors." Click.

I was overwhelmed and had started to itch. What "cuffs," what "minis"? I left the store in tears, searching desperately for the meds. "I am a Jewish princess…I know I am…I know I am."

I set out again the very next day with my mother in tow. After all, why not bring along the czar of shopping as support. At the first store, I stayed long enough to try on two pairs of pants. My shopping ADD kicked in and we left. The second store? I didn't even get as far as a dressing room before I dragged my mother by the hand out the door. "Mom, let's go, I hate everything!" I'm not sure she was completely in the car before I pulled away from the curb. Store three was the same scenario, only this time faster. Mom was getting dizzy from our pace. I offered her the meds.

By store four, I was dazed and prepared to face my fate. I wasn't a Princess because I didn't have a wardrobe worthy of the crown. Then, like a "once upon a time" moment, I spotted a consignment rack. A sexy little black dress called to me and I grabbed it. "Mine!" Was I on a roll? A fabulous jacket was next—so cool, so soft, so cheap! I was suddenly giddy. I did it; I shopped and purchased.

The crown was rightfully mine. But I still hate to shop.

I Paid $38 for a Dinner Roll

I HOLD A WORLD RECORD. YES, PROUDLY AND SADLY, I hold the world record for the highest price ever paid for a dinner roll. Not a Picasso, Monet, or Warhol but a puffy, slightly stale white roll. It cost $38.00. I'm broken, bankrupt and still hungry. How could something like this happen to the cheapest woman alive?

I went to a single's mixer. I have no idea what I was thinking; my better judgment was temporarily corrupted by the outlandish notion that someone would ask me to dance. The event was called for 6:00 p.m. at a local country club. No one in their right mind arrives at a party at the exact time it starts, right? I was born and raised on the "fashionably late" side of life.

I surmised my ETA should be 7:00. I shaved both legs, wore a fabulous little black dress and wobbled out of the house in my raspberry red Kate Spade high heels for the big event.

Always read an invitation carefully, which of course I didn't. Upon arrival, I noticed the woman selling tickets was wearing a cowgirl outfit.

"Oh no, was this a theme party?" I cried.

She said it was a Texas Holdem shindig but I looked into the room and thankfully no one was in western gear. I also noticed no one was standing up or mingling, just sitting sedately at tables talking amongst themselves.

"Excuse me, but where's the party?"

The women pointed to where I was looking. I was tempted to inquire if someone had died before I arrived. I paid the $38 admittance charge, asking one last time if I was headed in the right direction. She nodded. I felt ill. As I walked through the room, I was certain I was at a wake. These can't be my "peeps," I cried to myself. Was I in "The Twilight Zone?"

I desperately needed a drink and headed to the bar. I plopped down next to a man sitting alone at the far end and quickly pulled out the pen and paper I had brought as a security blanket in case no one talked to me. It was time to write and drink. I spent $8.00 for the house wine because the $38 didn't cover drinks. I determinedly headed over to the buffet; my ticket had to buy me something. Apparently not—I don't eat meat so the hamburgers were out. The flattened chicken pieces were looking greenish so forget that food group. All that was left was a basket of dinner rolls. I picked one up and placed it on my giant plate. Weak from hunger I walked back to the bar.

It was now 8:00 and the room was growing empty. "Wait, I just got here, don't go," I thought about yelling. "I even shaved my legs!"

I queried the man next to me who explained everyone arrived exactly at 6:00, mingled at the bar for twelve minutes and then sat down to eat. I think I burst into tears. "Who arrives on time? What happened to fashionably late? It's still early and if you all go I paid $38 for a roll!"

He tried to calm me down. Three people were dancing, which actually hurt my eyes as I watched them. Does rhythm leave your body at 65? By 8:15, we were almost the last two in the place.

I walked despondently to my car realizing I should have put at least a dozen rolls in my purse and only needed to shave one leg.

Let Me Eat Cake

RELIGION IS A TRICKY SUBJECT. I'm not a very religious person. Granted, I'll listen to thoughts about heaven, hell, and a higher being, but I am convinced God is not in the end zone, at the free throw line, or pushing someone's frozen ass up Mt. Everest. That is skill or luck, not religion. As for 25 virgins in heaven, I've yet to figure out why any man would want one, no less 25. If there were a reward in heaven, I would want chocolate cake.

I was reluctantly knee deep in a conversation about evolution vs. intelligent design when I had an epiphany. It suddenly struck me, an aha moment: Giorgio Armani is intelligent design. Who can resist his tailored elegance and sense of classicism? It's too expensive for me unless it's on sale, but nonetheless very intelligent.

Ralph Lauren is too predictable to be intelligent. He is consistent, and there's nothing stupid about a forest green cashmere crew neck, but it can also get a little boring.

There's hope however, because this fall's couture line looks fabulous. Everything is once again unaffordable but stunning and I encourage him keep it up.

Dolce and Gabbana have a long way to go by my definition of intelligent design. Ugh, Dolce and, ick, Gabbana. I don't get it. I know I'm supposed to, but I pull it off the rack and immediately shove it back. Sorry boys, not smart. Calvin Klein is always too big for me, although last season he had an amazing grey wool strapless party dress that brought tears to my eyes. Very close to a religious experience.

Marc Jacobs, are you intelligent? You're very, very close. I love most of your shoes and the purses are adorable, but can it really be intelligent if I can't afford the clothes? While I just say "no" to Prada, I confess that I have two pairs of Prada shoes and a purse my friend Tanni gave me instead of donating it. I will forever thank her for considering me her favorite charity and it hasn't left my shoulder in years. Jill Sander was intelligent. I say "was" because there is no guarantee intelligence is forever. I still believe spending $4,500 for a black jacket is insane.

My Donna Karan black cashmere coat showed extreme intelligence. It also saved me from a giant storage locker bill when I gave it to the girl who ran the facility. Intelligence on my part, also. I cannot forget Chanel, which is very close to heaven especially when Audrey Hepburn wore it.

Truthfully, at the end I really just want the chocolate cake.

To Tattoo or Not to Tattoo?

"TO TATTOO OR NOT TO TATTOO," that is my question. Everywhere I go and everyone I see has one or more. Not just a teeny tiny picture of a daisy on their shoulder, but arms, legs, and torsos covered in colorful ink. Who needs to go to The Art Institute when it's cheaper to stand on Michigan Ave. and look at the walking-people-paintings?

Truthfully, I'm a little jealous. Or am I? That's another good question. I haven't seen an 80-year old woman with a pirate on her upper arm yet but I bet she's out there. Maybe I could convince my mom to get a tattoo. She is a fashionista and determined even at 100 to keep up with the most current trends. Mom could be persuaded, especially if they had a fancy little tattoo counter at Saks. Maybe we could have a mother/daughter tattoo experience and then a nice lunch.

It seems very hip and cool to be one of the tattooed generation. I used to be hip and cool but it only involved long hair, bell-bottoms and a joint, not ink applied with a needle! Oh

God I'm a needle-phobe. Do they have defibrillators at tattoo parlors? And what would I want inscribed and where on my body would I want it? My head is about to explode from all the questions.

"Does anyone know where I left my cell phone?" might be a good choice for a tattoo as I would be hip and maybe someone knows. Ixnay to a flower image, as I don't need a further reminder that my plants are always on the brink of death. "Stand up straight" would be a tribute to Mom as would, "do you like your hair that color?"

It might be fun to be one of the tattooed folks because my hipness level dropped along with my hormones. I am worried, however, at how well an image will hold up as my arms wrinkle and sag. Regardless of the exactness of the original image, do they all ultimately become abstract paintings? Before I do anything, I need to check out an 80-old woman with a pirate on her arm.

Valentine's Day vs. New Year's Eve

UH OH, VALENTINE'S DAY IS LOOMING. I have the feeling of dread, much like I do on New Year's Eve. Are there two more pressure-packed days in the year than February 14 and December 31? I'm supposed to be happy and also have a date. Crap.

With only 48 hours to go, my anxiety builds. I think this feeling of dread started in grammar school. I'd have a 500-count pack of tiny little valentines and spend hours addressing them to my friends. We'd hang highly decorated bags on our desks and watched with baited breath as the teacher distributed the precious envelopes. "Oh no, so far I only have three and Barbara has ten!" I needed more cards in my bag or I'd die a thousand deaths. Isn't this too much pressure for a girl of eight?

It got worse. What if Jimmy didn't send me one card and I sent him nine? I loved him and what if he didn't love me? I'd have to quit 3rd grade. I'd be humiliated. I don't think I knew what that word meant but you get the idea. No wonder I'm still a wreck.

There is one thing I like about Valentine's Day—the candy. I used to love getting the tasteless but colorful tiny hearts with sayings on them like "you're nice" and "you're so cute." Now I'm afraid I'm not nice or cute, and terrified one of the little hearts could break my teeth. I opt for chocolates with soft centers—no caramel, nuts or toffee. I know my mom will send me a big frilly expensive card that barely fits in the mail box so by the time I pull it out it's folded in thirds or in shreds and I spend 15 minutes piecing it back together. Regardless, I'm relieved. I now only expect one card and not dozens.

With the pressure of the 14th rising and my happiness quotient dropping, I decide to spend Valentine's Day under cover and ruminate about the humiliation of New Year's Eve. BTW, I finished 3rd grade.

Bad Date Hall of Fame Awards

I HAVE A BAD DATE HALL OF FAME. It's also known as my personal pantheon of duds. I'm not happy to make this announcement as obviously it means I had a really crappy time and wasted a perfectly good evening I could have spent with a box of Raisinets watching *America's Got Talent.* I don't hold a yearly induction ceremony, but sometimes it is quite a struggle determining who will raise up the "best bad date statue" on December 31. Sadly, there's usually a runner-up candidate, and as a safety net, a third runner-up, so my voting can go right down to the wire. One year there was a man I fondly referred to as Hannibal Lecter, but I still had my liver, so he didn't make the final cut. He tried so hard to win but only one prize per year.

I'd like to remind my new inductee that women have been given the right to vote. There have been three female Secretaries of State, one Speaker of the House, one Oprah, three Supreme Court Justices, one President of Harvard.

Catch my drift? The best advice to my dud date is to let the woman you're out with, speak. We are a legitimate gender and can kick some serious ass.

I met my award winning date at a bar for a drink and from the moment I arrived, he did not stop talking. Yap, yap, yap, yap and not about politics, sports, movies, or even weather, which would have been comic relief and perhaps interesting. His favorite subject was himself. Ironically, a movie did come to mind: *My Dinner with Andre.* Andre Gregory wove tales of his adventures both spiritual and real while Wallace Shawn sat at dinner and listened. His life journey was mesmerizing and the time flew as he talked.

That was not my evening. It didn't even seem to matter if I was there. I began to wonder if I was. Didn't he notice I had not said a word for two hours; it felt like six. You know you are having a really bad time if fainting or bloodletting becomes a reasonable option as a way to end the date. I thought about screaming, "Just shut up" at the top of my lungs; I thought about it a lot. I realized however, as I listened to the life story of every single boring family member, why bother straining my voice, as someday I might go on a date where I needed it. When the bartender brought the final bill, I ripped my half out of my wallet, said thank you and ran to my car.

"Mr. I'm So Interesting," congratulations—you won hands down. Time to start next year's list and stock up on Raisinets.

III.
Where?

Lounge Lizards and Me

REPTILES CREEP ME OUT. They are slimy, slithery and scary. As a child, I was forced to go in the Reptile House at the zoo because my parents wouldn't let me wait outside alone. I was pissed. I walked around with my eyes squinted half shut. There were lizards longer than my dad's car and their skin looked a lot like Mom's purse. I thought as an adult that I had left lizards behind.

"Gail, it will be fun; get dressed and come with us to Sullivan's," my girlfriend Brenda pleaded. Sullivan's is a pick-up bar and restaurant. No one has ever picked me up in a bar. I was a bad bar person. I lacked the knack of casual conversation and was brunette. I always brought a book so I had something to do when I was passed by for a blonde. I stayed home a lot.

"Please come. It's happy hour so the food and drinks are half price," Brenda insisted.

"What time should we meet?" I'm genetically incapable of resisting half price. Thanks Dad.

Sullivan's was packed with men staring at scantily clad women. I was wearing a sweater so I knew I'd get plenty of reading done. As I scanned the crowded room, I couldn't help but notice the average age of the men looked about 65. Shouldn't they be home collecting Social Security or making doctor's appointments? I had never seen older guys cruising for women. It was surreal. Where were the hotties with hair and flat abs? I witnessed a man at least 80 draped over a 50ish looking woman, staring down her low-cut dress at her breasts and never once coming up for air. I suddenly had the urge to read.

"Brenda, do you smell something funny? My eyes are watering. And who are these guys?"

"These guys? They're a bunch of Lounge Lizards," she replied as she sniffed the air and made a face.

Crap. I was in a room of reptiles.

"Hi girls," I heard from behind my stool. We both whipped around to see a man walking toward us. He stared at Brenda (she's blonde) and casually put his arm on the back of her chair. I reached into my purse for my book. "What's going on, ladies?"

He wasn't talking to me. My eyes, however, were beginning to itch from the nasty cologne he was wearing. As he ogled Brenda, I studied our guest Lizard. He was approximately 65 with leathery skin from too much desert sun, wearing a green polyester shirt open to mid-chest, and his dull thinning blonde hair was slicked straight back and glistening from too much gel. His eyes seemed to pop out of his head when he spoke. He looked slithery and like Mom's purse.

I scrutinized the room pretending to be Jane Goodall studying this animal called the Lounge Lizard in his natural habitat. I noticed they were resilient and when rejected did not pull out a book, but moved immediately on to the next woman. They were determined and undeterred creatures hell-bent to find someone who accepted their offer of a free drink. It was a numbers game for these slithering creatures. They seemed to stalk their prey alone and had no compunction about butting in on a fellow predator's action. Crafty and rude, they persevered. Meanwhile our slimy guy was moving closer and closer to Brenda's right ear.

"Want to have dinner with me Sunday night?" he whispered.

I had to eavesdrop for the purpose of science.

"No thank you, I have a boyfriend" she politely replied.

"I don't care, have dinner with me," he insisted. Like I said, resilient, but shouldn't a mountain lion come down and eat him now?

I quickly grew tired of studying Lizards and had finished my book. I decided next time I'd skip "happy hour" and go directly to the zoo.

"No, No. Anything but the Car Keys!"

HAPPY 90TH BIRTHDAY, DAD. He turned 90 even though he's been telling people for the last three years he's 90. He's the only person I know that lies upward. My mother has been tweaking her age as long as I've known her. Rumor has it she has two drivers licenses with different ages. Knowing Mom, she might even have more than one birth certificate. She's a trickster.

I've followed faithfully in her footsteps since I was 40. Until 40, I bragged upwards every year as people never thought I looked my age. Thirty was a breeze. "Yes I'm 30 and I don't give a damn," was my attitude. Then along came 40 and I went into hiding right after the birthday cake. "I can't possibly be 40," I would cry myself to sleep. My friend Bob had to do an "age intervention." He dragged me out of bed to go out and drink.

I didn't give Dad a present yet because he returns all gifts, even pastries, which I thought he couldn't bring back, but he found a way. The very best gift he received was from the Department of Motor Vehicles of Illinois. Ya gotta love their generosity. The DMV renewed my dad's driver's license for his birthday. Now my present to everyone who lives near Dad is telling them to stay home and off the roads. This includes all the folks who like to shop at Nordstrom's and Neiman Marcus because he drives my mother there a lot. Why didn't we take his keys away you might ask yourself? We did and even sold his car but when no one was looking, he tricked us, went out and bought a new one. He's crafty.

The worst part is I know the day will come when my son is standing in front of me requesting the car keys. "No, anything but the keys," I'll scream, clutching them in my hand and running or by then, crawling out the door. Take my good china that's never seen a morsel of food, my silver which is still in the tarnish proof packaging, my Tiffany wine and champagne glasses, but not the car." I'm sure he'll be gentle and consoling as he chases me down the street, bribing me back with cab fares or a bus pass. Will I hand them over? You bet your sweet ass I won't. So Dad, on your 90th birthday all I can say is "run!"

What's so Happy about Happy Hour?

I CONFESS IT WAS HEARTBREAKING. Call me shallow, superficial, vain and obviously delusional, but I never thought a bartender could ruin my life. I was happily sitting at the bar of my Seattle hotel, sipping a mediocre yet expensive Sauvignon Blanc, looking out at the incredible view across the water and gleefully anticipating my longed-for salmon dinner. I was in a cute little black dress, strappy high heels, had put on makeup, blown dry my hair and shaved my legs. Yes, both of them as sometimes I lose interest by the second and once actually skipped it. I was thinking I looked pretty cute.

After ordering my second glass of wine, three twenty-something blonde girls walked up to the bar to pay their tab. They were "hotties." I would kill for their wrinkle-free complexions or milky skin tone. No Botox or fillers for these youngsters. The bartender proceeded to tell them about "happy hour and free champagne on Saturday," practically pleading with them to come back and bring their friends.

"Excuse me, I'll still be at the hotel on Saturday," I wanted to blurt out. Was I chopped liver? Was I invisible or did I remind him of his nana?

Then it struck me. This was exactly like the moment I realized no one called me "miss" anymore. One day out of the clear blue, I was "ma'am." Presto chango, I was dubbed "ma'am." "You talking to me? I'm not a "ma'am, I CAN'T BE "MA'AM; anything but ma'am." Aren't I too young? I needed a mirror, the witness protection program, a plastic surgeon. My mother is a "ma'am." The older woman over there, but not me. The loss of "miss" was a milestone. Do men suffer this way?

And now I became too old for happy hour? This couldn't be happening. Hey, life-ruining bartender, more wine. Suddenly I had lost my desire for salmon. Then he turned to me and smiled. Aha, the guy obviously forgot to tell me about Saturday. I felt relieved and much, much better, all that anxiety for nothing.

"Ma'am, would you like to close out your tab?"

Bye-bye Bergdorfs

IS YOUR BANK ACCOUNT GETTING YOU DOWN? Mine was. I was feeling sad and longing for the days of mocha Frappuccinos and soy lattes. I had to say good-bye to those expensive coffee drinks, to say nothing of manicures and $10 martinis with blue cheese-stuffed olives. How I longed for those tasty olives.

To make matters more dire, according to my budget it would be 2020 before I could buy anything new to wear. Call it shabby chic or threadbare but I won't be looking good and I'm definitely not making my own clothes. Face it, no one over 50 can see well enough to thread a needle. Last time I tried, I had to get a tetanus shot when the bleeding stopped.

Hang on; maybe I will have new clothes before 2020. It could happen. There on the horizon in giant red letters was my salvation: TARGET! It's the new Bergdorfs!

The store is packed with people; shopping carts are flying in every direction. I didn't know you could buy a dress for $19.95. Kiss Neimans good-bye and try on one of these babies. Who cares about the crappy lighting in the hard-to-find dressing rooms; I'm talking under $20. I admit I burst into tears looking at myself under florescent lights but I almost bought a dress. Sadly, it would have looked much better on someone 17 years old but happily, I could have paid cash for it.

Maybe life won't be so bad after all. Frappuccinos are way too fattening and soy lattes are chalky tasting and ridiculously expensive. As for my beloved blue cheese olives, how hard can it be to stuff an olive without stabbing myself?

Besides, I had a tetanus shot.

I Abdicated my Throne for a Bowl of Chili

MY STREAK ENDED. IT'S A BITTERSWEET MOMENT when you break a streak regardless of the dubious achievement of having attained it. My "Queen of One Date" title has been revoked by virtue of the fact that I went on a second date. Curses. I had become royalty in my own mind, although I didn't have the appropriate clothes or jewelry. I think an ermine collar on a red robe would be necessary, along with a 20-pound tiara.

Not having been asked on a second date in six months, my knee-jerk reaction when suddenly and surprisingly invited was an immediate "yes." I should have deliberated far more carefully and weighed the options. Date? Queen status? It's not every girl that gets to be royal, even if it's for being a dating loser.

My "streak-ending" date invited me over for turkey chili. Yes, read this and weep. I surrendered the crown for a lousy bowl of beans. I was nervous about going over to a veritable stranger's house for a second date. I received endless warnings and advice: "don't go", "meet in a public place" and "bring mace, a gun, brass knuckles or sharp stick."

I was worried and weaponless but went. I arrived hungry and after the obligatory house tour, I looked around for pre-dinner appetizers. Sweaty and a bit hypoglycemic, I was desperate for a cracker. He handed me a glass of wine but zip in the form of food. He wanted to talk about art and I wanted a vitamin B12 shot to stay conscious. Sadly and boringly, I gave him the art history lecture I've heard myself say a million times, having been an art dealer for 24 years. I might have dozed off after Impressionism. I know I lost him during Warhol.

And speaking of Campbell soup cans, I needed soup or anything as I was about to keel over. Finally, I declared I wanted dinner. He took out two bowls and filled them with chili from a very tiny pot on the stove. Mr. Streak-Breaker then put the pot in the sink, as it was empty! Next, he placed between us the smallest loaf of bread I've ever seen. I think I served bigger loaves when I played tea party with my dolls. I scarfed down the beans and two pieces of bread. There was nothing more, dinner over. Dessert was only something about which I could dream or stop and buy on my way home.

My title relinquished for a bowl of chili. I've asked my Facebook friends if date two could be annulled but the majority ruled it counted. I learned the hard way there is nothing like being royalty regardless of how you get the crown.

National Holidays Got You Down? Eat Pez and Drink.

BAH HUMBUG, ANOTHER LONG HOLIDAY WEEKEND looms on the horizon. Didn't we just have the 4th of July? Personally, I think they should be spaced much farther apart as once again the pressure to grill or be invited to a barbecue mounts. I don't have a grill or the mental fortitude to buy one when a deadline is involved. It makes me nervous and itchy to be in a rush. I have considered purchasing a small George Foreman model for the kitchen counter but I think size does matter on national holidays. Besides which, even if I had a big snazzy tricked out Weber then I'd need guests to invite over. Is there a "guest" category on Craig's List? All my friends know they could be blown up or set on fire if I'm cooking. I can't send out invitations that say, "wear fire retardant clothing."

I am a good guest, however, so if anyone needs an extra at their barbecue I'm available. Although please don't ask me to bring a "dish." I never know what that really means—a dish of what? And does preparing one require gingham clothing? Why can't I just bring a box of Oreos or pass out Pez? On second thought, don't invite me. I'll have holiday fun by going to a parade with the dog. He loves marching bands and taking hot dogs from small children. I'll just be happy I'm not home blowing up the deck or setting my friends on fire.

I think it's best to be alone. I'll drink bottles of nice, crispy Sauvignon Blanc, eat Pez and read the back issues of *People* that I borrowed from my dentist's office. I promised I'd bring them back on Tuesday.

This Blonde Didn't Have More Fun

BLONDES DON'T HAVE MORE FUN, at least this blonde didn't. I tried, but fun wasn't in the cards. Blondes are a phenomenon I've never understood. I grew up a brunette, a color that received very little attention. Trust me, when a brunette walks in a room not one male head turns. Business continues as usual, blah, blah, blah, the conversations go on as if nothing happened. Enter a woman with flaxen hair and like clockwork, every head turns her way. The air is virtually sucked out of the place and life comes to a standstill while little blondie strolls by. It never fails. Never. I know this because I was the girl with long brown hair who went unnoticed. I'm not trying to evoke sympathy, just seeking to understand this force of nature. "Hey I'm over here, I may have brown hair but I have big blue eyes. Is that chicken liver?" But alas not much action came my way.

Ironically, I've never been attracted to men with blonde hair. Nope, I liked the tall dark type; the fair-haired boys never turned my head. They still don't, although my man demographic is gray or bald so it's a moot point.

I didn't become blonde to experience more popularity but to mask becoming gray. My mom pointed out to me that, perhaps, I should do something about my newly arrived gray hairs as they made me look old. "Thanks, Mom, and excuse me while I go hide from public view." Before I knew it, my brown locks were gone. I was blondish and also out $120 every five weeks. An expensive proposition for a person who takes back roads to avoid the tollbooth. I've changed colorists five times but nothing changed when I walked in a room. "Hey, I'm almost blonde, look over here!" Nothing. Had I vanished? Truthfully, after four years and five colorists, I didn't care about the turning of bald or gray heads. I missed my dark brown hair. It went better with my eyes and checkbook.

I'll Have What She's Having

I HAVE A PSYCHOLOGICAL DISORDER. Many of my friends have speculated about this for years, and in my defense, they were presumptuous. I've checked the "Diagnostic and Statistical Manual of Mental Disorders" and my problem is not mentioned. It's either not officially recognized, not taken seriously by psychiatrists or I'm the first person to exhibit symptoms and give it a name. It falls under the general category of "envy" and it's not for a penis. I don't know what Freud was smoking when he thought up that idea. I've never wanted one of my own. A pair of Manolos or Jimmy Choos, but not a penis. My problem is more troubling yet I'm too humiliated to seek counseling.

I have "order envy." Yes, it's a real issue. I never order right in a restaurant. I look longingly at what is on everyone else's plate and despairingly at mine. It makes me sad and costs money.

My friend Betsy has a perfect record when it comes to getting the best thing on the menu. It never fails; I always want what she's having. So, why don't I follow her lead? This question haunts me. For example, she gets a fresh farm-veggie omelet and do I order the same thing? No, I ask for the turkey sandwich after sweating with indecision. Out comes her fluffy, yummy looking eggs and my thinly sliced, fake turkey. I'm green with envy as I pick at my loser choice and fight back tears.

"What are you getting?" is my restaurant mantra. I query everyone at the table and carefully consider their answers. The pressure mounts as I insist on ordering last and the waiter is impatiently hovering over me waiting for my selection and my friends are giving me dirty looks because they're hungry and I'm torn between Emily's choice of curried chicken and Les's order of trout. "I can't decide!" I want to shout and seek medical attention, but don't. Then it never fails; the ill-fated yet predictable words come out of my mouth as I choose the usual suspect. "Salmon."

Men on Sale at Match.com

I HATE TO SHOP, NO LESS SHOPPING DURING A BIG SALE when the stores are mobbed with crazed psycho bargain hunters. "Last Call" at Neimans almost sent me back to therapy. I was dazed, confused and sweaty rifling through the endless racks of merchandise and started to question my sexuality. My mother, however, is an "extreme" shopper. I witnessed her dive and actually disappear into a pile of clothes and appear ten minutes later waving a black sweater. She has no fear and very good lung capacity.

I am also cheap, which is a catch-22, as I disdain shopping yet am tempted by a sale. So when I saw Match.com was running one, I decided to try it again. Men on sale—now that sounded a lot better than retail.

In my experience, I always ended up returning "full" priced men. Yet in my heart of hearts, what could I expect from a "marked down" man? Was it "last call" at Match.com? Everyone must go to make room for the new winter line of guys? I got nervous thinking the remainder bin would be filled with short, beefy and bald. But like I said, I'm cheap so I clicked "join." Any seasoned shopper would have rolled up her sleeves and started plowing through the profiles. Armed with antacids and Cabernet, I judiciously read through the emails that came my way. I mistrusted misspellings, poor sentence structure and use of the so-called word "irregardless" as I knew these sale boys were not for an English major. I handpicked a few marked down guys and ventured out for wine or coffee. I hoped against all odds that there was a forgotten "Armani" man left at the bottom of the bin and if I could be like Mom and dive down there, I'd find him.

Ah yes, I quickly remembered why I don't shop sales. I remember when I originally joined Match two years ago. There was "Appetizer Man" who ate them all himself and didn't ask why I wasn't eating as he was too busy wanting to know if I had money or assets. "Mr. Cock-eyed Conservative" repeatedly called Berkeley, Bezerkely. "Goldfinger" wore more jewelry at one time than I have ever owned. "Mr. Whoopsie I Forgot" wrote we had so much in common that I should call him. I emailed back to remind him he took me out two years ago—had he become senile in the interim? I especially liked "No Eye Contact Man" who was so busy looking around, he wouldn't have noticed had I left. I did get a lovely flattering note from a man my son's age. Not remotely tempting, for fear he might slip and call me "Mom." This was too Oedipal even for an English major.

The sale ends in January but I have shopping fatigue just thinking about joining. I hope Mom isn't too disappointed that I don't have the lung capacity or nerve to dive into a sale bin again. I think I prefer shopping at Neimans to shopping for men.

Bedroom Crime Scene

I HATE BUGS. SO IMAGINE MY SHOCK AND HORROR when I walked into my bedroom and there on the floor was a crusty creature as big as a lobster. Yes, I swear it was a lobster-size insect.

I screamed. It lay there. I ran around in a circle not knowing what to do. "Oh my God, oh my God" was all I could choke out as I spun around. I called frantically for my trusty yellow Labrador retriever "Potato" and his mighty Australian shepherd sidekick "Wiggie" for backup. Surely one of my furry boys would go after the giant bug and save the day.

"Wiggie, get 'em boy." Nothing. He took a sniff and left the room. I thought I could appeal to Potato's love of anything edible. "Go Potato go, he looks yummy."

The dog would eat toxic waste yet could not work up an appetite for my uninvited guest.

I was cursed, totally grossed out and started to feel frantic. But aha, I had one last weapon in my animal arsenal…

the cat! "Missie, come quick I need your feline ferocity." She stared at me and walked the other way.

What was I to do? Should I kill it or name it? I had to get in my room to sleep. I thought about just packing up and moving. My blood pressure was dropping rapidly yet I knew I had to act. It's lobster-creature or me, which briefly reminded me of the scene in "Annie Hall" when the lobster got loose on the kitchen floor but that was funnier. This felt more like "High Noon." (If anyone reading is an insect-hugger, stop reading now).

I was barefoot. I needed a weapon. A baseball bat would have been perfect or musket but no such luck, just a shoe was available. It was me and the shoe, poised to act. I didn't know if my cute Kate Spade open-toed sandal could crush the creature in one blow and I was right...couldn't. Argh. It got ugly and quite messy but I persevered.

I now had a crime scene on my hands. Yes, I probably watch too much TV as I envisioned the police taping around the body and asking for witnesses. I was sure the cat would squeal and send me off in an orange jumpsuit.

As I threw out the untidy remains, I sadly realized I would never be able to eat lobster again.

I Feel Better About My Face, Neck and Finances!

I FEEL TEN YEARS YOUNGER THAN MY BIRTH CERTIFI-CATE. My question is whether it's better to "feel" or "look" younger. That's a tough one. I have to pick "feel" because I can't afford "look."

I returned the skin care products I irrationally purchased that cost more than my rent. It would be ridiculous to be homeless with only a new age cellular skin repair cream and eye rejuvenator to my name. Besides my brain was hurting from trying to figure out the mathematical possibilities of paying the huge Neiman's bill that would soon be in my sweaty, trembling hand. Should I pay it in full and see how long I could go hungry? No, I had dinner plans. I figured out installments in $10, $25, $50 and $100 increments and realized I might not live long enough to be out of debt. I toyed with going to my grave having an outstanding Neiman's balance but tragically, it would then be my son's only inheritance. I would be a bad mom memory.

I want to personally thank my girlfriends who called and gave me the courage to march back to the makeup counter and just say no. The eye cream really did make my eyes burn, and the moisturizer turned my skin an odd shade of red, so I felt I had a case for a refund. Guilt looms too large in my life. It's a Jewish curse. I think God must have said to the Jews, "Go forth and feel guilty, be sure to multiply, and of course, shop." I hope that meant for shoes!

There was no need for all my angst as the salesgirls couldn't have been nicer and promptly gave me a refund. I felt the years melt away. I peeked in the mirror; the years were still there. Let's just say my inner self felt younger and I had more money. Triumphantly on my way out, it took every ounce of strength to resist the shoe department, which was calling to me from the 2nd floor. I stared up longingly with tears in my eyes, but didn't go.

I didn't leave empty handed, though. There is a trick, a foolproof way to spare oneself the defeat of returns. To think I could have avoided days of buyer's remorse and boring my friends to death talking about moisturizer. Get samples! You can test drive the products. Mom, queen of makeup counters from here to Manhattan, why didn't you tell me this? I came home toting tiny jars of skin creams, puffiness-reducing eye products and miracle lotions for my wrinkled neck. A bag of "promise" was mine and it was free.

Sex, Prunes and the Sahara

RECENTLY, ON A MATCH.COM DATE, a 76-year old man asked me if women over 60 still want to have sex. Strangely, he stated on his profile that he was 66; funny math I'd say. And men protest that women fudge the numbers! Geez.

Hearing his query, I had to wonder if he was having a stroke or was that his best "line" to get me in bed. Should I rip off my blouse and jump up yelling, "Yes, yes, yes I will prove we do" or call an ambulance? I stared to see if his mouth was drooping as he continued. He explained that his friends have told him menopausal and post-menopausal women turn into shriveled up prunes drier than the Sahara. Hmmm, his friends are well-traveled and constipated. He also cited that he had never slept with a woman over 60 as his ex-wife was 20 years younger than he. How's that for seduction? Hot or not?

Mother Nature does play a cruel trick on women. Just when the kids are gone or we finally have some free time for hot sex, our hormones say "you had a good run." Desire still reigns, but so long to dewy skin, thick hair, a waistline, a good night's sleep and yes, lubrication. Ouch. I admit I wasn't prepared for this sleight of hand, and shock with no "awe" seemed to be my future.

To add insult to injury, Big Pharma flooded the market with blue "M&M's"—Viagra. The years when men were supposed to be in sexual sync with women were—POOF—gone in a nanosecond. Prescriptions in hand, the old guys came roaring back to life. A veritable stampede of bulging stomachs, balding heads, neckless, chinless and wrinkled men were wondering if I was a dried up prune and if so, would I get out of their way as younger models certainly were anxiously awaiting. (Got big bucks, boys?)

Apparently, my prudishness has become the aforementioned *prunishness*. Armed with my game changing personal version of WD40, I would definitely say "yes" if I met an age appropriate man to whom I was attracted. It's a lot like the vast, empty, desolate landscape of the Sahara out there in my man-land. Prune Danish anyone?

I like Wine and to Whine

"I'm mad as hell, and I'm not going to take this anymore!"
—Howard Beale, *Network*

WINE BY THE GLASS IS TOO EXPENSIVE! I'm sick of paying as much for a glass as an oil change. Has anyone else noticed this bar and restaurant sleight of hand? I'd like to see a glass under $9.00, wouldn't you? And if by chance it is cheap, we're talking toxic waste. I remember when a nice pinot noir was $5.50; not any more—got $12.00? These days I madly search the menu for a wine I can afford and don't care about the color, just the price. Tears well up in my eyes realizing beer would better serve my saving for retirement. But I hate beer and put my head down on the bar sobbing.

It was like a dream come true when I discovered malbec—lovely, Argentinean and cheap. I stopped crying. At $7.00 a glass, I could once again fantasize about retirement. I spotted it on enough menus to keep me happy, high and able to leave a tip. I smirked as my friends ordered the expensive pinot and cabernet while I mumbled my malbec order so they couldn't hear. The grape was mine alone. And then it wasn't. My secret wine caught on and now it's at least $10.00 a glass and I'm drinking Amstel light.

My friend Jane turned me on to riesling, which is reasonably priced and it isn't insulin sweet if you order correctly. I initially thought the grape was for wine wimps, losers with unsophisticated taste buds and restricted nasal passages. I was wrong. I could learn to love again and retire.

Now I'm begging, order the malbec.

No Cooking Required

I HAVE NO NEW YEAR'S RESOLUTIONS. Oh wait, I do. I resolve to have sex in the kitchen. Does anyone do this? It's never mentioned in the conversations I've had with my girlfriends about the strangest places you've ever had sex. I've heard pool table, bunny hill, public beach and elevator but never kitchen. It stays on my list because I don't need to lose weight, which is on all my friends' lists. I desperately need alternative resolutions as thankfully all my jeans fit. I have a lot of problems but none of them have to do with eating less.

Let me think; next year I could be nicer, but then my friends would worry I was sick and dying. It's better to remain a little cranky and neurotic for their sake. I could whine less, but whhhhhy. I could spend more time in the grocery store. Again I have to ask myself why, when I've perfected the one meal at a time lifestyle. I could drink less wine but that would just be stupid. I could go to more movies but that requires paying for parking. I could get a colonoscopy.

It is a popular event in my peer group, actually more than going to the movies. It would make my doctor happy but then what would he nag me about? Imagine how cranky and whiny I would be before I drink all that horrid liquid. I would actually have to be dragged crying and screaming all the way to the procedure. I hear the drugs they give you are pretty great but drugs are so 1970s.

It looks like I have one tentative and one for-sure resolution. I'm iffy on the colonoscopy. I know I should and it costs about the same as a movie with a large popcorn and Coke. However, sex in the kitchen doesn't require money, shopping or cooking. It's a keeper.

Queen of One Date Tells All

"SAM, YOU HAVE TO HELP ME!" I cried into the phone.

"What is it, babe? Try and calm down and tell me what's wrong."

"I don't get it; I've become the "QUEEN OF ONE DATE." Yep, I gave myself a new title. "Jewish Princess" was out. Although I liked the promotion to Queen, the rest of it sucked.

"What are you talking about?"

"Well, I think that kind of summed it up. I never get asked on a second date. One date and I'm out. I don't get it; no one calls again. Why? What should I do? Or what did I do?"

"Don't talk," he responded without hesitation.

"Huh?" Was he talking to me or about me?

"Don't talk when you go out with these men. Just listen."

"Huh?"

"Let the guy talk his brains out; don't compete with him."

"I don't get it. Just sit there like a lump?"

"Just sit there and smile. Or ask a question."

"Huh?"

"Ask a question about him. Men like soft and sweet."

"Excuse me?" I think all the blood was rushing dangerously to my head.

"Gail, you don't get it." He was right; I was faint, developing a rash and didn't get it.

"What about a conversation?" I whispered as I began to lose consciousness.

"Men have competition all day in business and don't want it with a woman during down time."

"Is a conversation competition?"

"See how you are? You're challenging me and I'm giving you advice." He was serious. I was suddenly feeling faint and stepped out onto the patio for air.

"So we're talking about an evening where I'm just smiling and asking my date questions about himself? There's no conversation where two people equally exchange thoughts. Is that what you're saying?"

"That's what I'm saying honey."

"And if I do that I'll get to go on a second date?"

"That's right."

"Well, thanks for the advice." I wasn't sure I really meant it.

"Let me know how it goes."

I laid down on the cold cement and stared up at the dark sky realizing I couldn't follow Sam's advice. Could he really be right? I had to choose a vow of smiling silence or forever maintain my title of "Queen of One Date?"

Royalty is so much better than dating.

Call 911 and Get a Husband!

"WHAT WOULD YOU DO IF YOU FOUND ME face down on the bathroom floor?"

A 68-year-old man I was dating asked me this over a perfectly nice glass of cabernet. Talk about ruining the moment and my next sip. I was incredulous and almost spit it out but I really hate wasting wine. As for his question, "huh?" was my first response.

"What would you do if you found me face down on the bathroom floor," he repeated.

Why not the kitchen, I pondered. It suddenly hit me that he was serious and there was a right answer. Oh no, was this a test of my emergency medical skills or a marriage proposal? Did I want to marry him and if so, could I get him off the floor in time for the justice of the peace to arrive before his lawyer came with a prenup? It would take skill but I could do it.

"Ummmmm," I stalled for time, composure and another glass of wine.

Then it dawned on me. This is how men over 60 propose. If you answer right, you get the ring. Fear of commitment has been replaced by fear of "face down." Talk about a light bulb moment.

Rick, a 65-year-old man I met, told me he was "sick, sick, sick" of dating. He didn't want to spend another moment alone; 37 years was enough. He was ready to marry for the fourth time, and seemed hell bent on getting there from the tone of his voice. Hang on there, little buddy, after 37 years of dating, why now? Could it be fear of "face down?"

Think of how many men are out there living in terror. If you have any nursing skills or know CPR, now is the time to find a husband. And if you want Rick's phone number let me know, but FYI, his third marriage lasted nine days.

As for my date, I answered the "face down" question incorrectly so I'm still single. "Call a travel agent" was funny but not the response he was looking for. I'm guessing "dial 911 and administer CPR until the ambulance arrives" gets the ring. P.S. He subsequently married the next woman; she was a nurse.

First Read The Manual!

I COULDN'T FIND THE OWNER'S MANUAL to my car, which makes it impossible for me to change my clock to Central Standard Time. I desperately needed the directions or I'd be stuck in Pacific Standard Time forever and subsequently late for everything.

Then I had the big aha moment: Think how much easier life would be if we all came with an operating manual. Our own personal book of instructions; it's genius! Don't ask me any more questions, just read the manual. Think of the people you would never have dated, married or slept with—a real time and money saver.

No hiding the truth about what a raving lunatic you are before chugging that first cup of coffee—how you sleep with your socks on, that blonde isn't your real hair color, you cannot self-serve at the gas station, or you are looking for a kidney donor for your cat. It would all be explained in the manual. The beauty of this brings tears to my eyes.

The people who don't run off screaming at the end would be either a retired Special Ops guy nostalgically looking for a search and destroy mission, or someone as crazy as you are.

Personally, I think I'd attract a lot of Special Ops men. For starters, the hardest part for me would be age disclosure. Sorry Mom, I might have to give up my vow of silence. Then, I'm the aforementioned raving lunatic before coffee, and after coffee but not après a glass of wine nine hours later. I know this begs a lot of cranky time. Is anyone still reading?

I don't eat until noon, so ixnay me if you like to go out for breakfast or want me to whip up some pancakes. While we're on food, stop reading if you don't like to eat dinner out or don't believe the cocktail hour is spiritual.

I've lost more readers.

There would be a short chapter devoted to bedding and snoring, and also ticking clocks. I must have ridiculously high thread count sheets, *absofreakinglutely* no snoring and all ticking silenced. Oh God, no one will read to the end, will they?

Hold on a second, here's a really good chapter: "I Hate Shopping." Oh wait, another great read is, "I love sports, watch the entire NCAA Men's Basketball Tournament and listen to ESPN radio."

I'm guessing three Special Ops guys are trying to find me.

Sex and the Elephant

WATCH OUT FOR THE ELEPHANT. That big old creature in the living room called, "we never have sex." Is there anyone who hasn't heard those words? Hear that complaint enough and it becomes like white noise. "Blah, blah, blah. Enough."

I read in the New York Times that the "we never have sex bar" has been reset. It now ranges from "never" to 365 days in a row thanks to Brad and Charla Muller or 101 days in a row, thanks to Doug and Annie Brown. Is "thanks" the word I'm searching for? Don't look at me; I've learned to walk and vacuum around the big gray elephant in my living room. But what better way to perk up the old dull marriage than "I think we should have sex every night for a year, if that's good for you." Is there a man alive who would say no? Annie opted for a "conservative" 101 days but regardless, I think we have an Olympic event here. Can you say 2020 Winter Games?

I admit I would never have thought of record-setting days of sex as a solution to shooing the pachyderm out of the room. Divorce was my answer to animal control. A big hot affair is a way to end sex on the home front that I like to call "The Elliot Spitzer School of Marriage Therapy." This is popular in the 'old guys looking for young wives circles', but it's costly and usually ends in another divorce.

Brenda and Annie, you are kickass wives. I read the average couple has sex 66 times a year and I'm still pondering if that seems like too much or too little. Then again, I really like elephants.

Little Bo Peep and Her Sleep Deprived Sheep

I WILL OFFER A SMALL REWARD to any couple that can get a good night's sleep on a queen size bed. I don't believe it's possible to wake up cognizant or able to do simple addition when sleeping together on such a small space. The bed is just too damn tiny. And don't protest with the "cozy" argument as I think what you really mean is cramped.

Cuddling is sweet, but face it, three minutes is the maximum cuddle time and then it's "every man for himself." Staking out territory involves skill and speed. I like to sprawl around looking for the exact spot to claim. I need to move. I need to stretch out. I refuse to be caught in the upper left hand corner with my right arm hanging off the side turning blue from lack of circulation and rapidly losing feeling in my left leg. That sweet person with whom I was just snuggling needs to move over or be smothered.

Admittedly, I'm a bit of the "Princess and the Pea" type, as a good night's sleep involves hundreds of stars to be in perfect alignment. I can't survive without my two almost featherless pillows scrunched under my head. I've had them since I was a teenager and never travel or move without them. Admittedly, they could disintegrate at any moment but fit nicely in my purse. My sheets must have a thread count of more than 480, and yes, I do know if they're 479. And anything that ticks, hums, or vibrates must be stifled or smashed to smithereens.

Then there's snoring. I'd like to meet the person who can sleep through the night with a snorer. My girlfriend told me she crams pillows over her husband's head to muffle the noise. I think a hammer is the better solution. It's clear I'm going to end up alone.

A king size bed is the only hope for two people to survive. It's like your own planet with room to move about freely, vote on reasonable borders and meet in the middle for drinks, sex, the three-minute cuddle or a spelling bee. When you queen size lovers are done counting sheep and alert enough, come collect your reward.

I Hate Reality TV More than *The New Yorker*

I HATE, HATE, HATE REALITY TV. Yes, even more than *The New Yorker* and packing boxes. Reality television is like a roach infestation; it multiplies with each passing day. Every hour and on every channel, someone else's reality is in my face. My world is real enough; I don't need a total stranger's problems, too. Who cared about the last *Survivor*? I have my own survival issues and they don't have to do with eating scorpions in a bikini. My reality TV show would be called, "Crap, my rent is due" or "Who wants my dental bill?"

Btw, is "The Bachelor" still looking for a wife? That would be really depressing because if the nubile young creatures they prance in front of him can't get a man there's no hope for the rest of us. Girls, get a grip, ditch the bachelor and do some long range career planning because there's a 50% chance you will be single again and possibly poor. As for losing weight in prime time, why is this a TV show? My best advice is to ditch the Big Mac with cheese and pull out of the drive-thru line or hand it to "America's Next Top Model" before she evaporates.

I have a great idea for Baby Boomer reality TV: "What Would You Trade to be 40 Again?" This is imaginative and very dark programming in my book. Hmm, let me think, there's Mom. No, I would only trade her to be 30. Now that's TV with a touch of *The Hunger Games*. In truth, 40 sounds really good and looks even better: smooth skin, no wrinkles, no grey hair, plenty of hormones and a sex drive.

I'd like real people to get off my screen. Eat scorpions, lose weight, find husbands and become models on your own time. And I should call Mom in case she reads this and is searching for her passport.

Face Down

MY FRIEND JOHN TOLD ME HE KNOWS what women fear most. He insisted that we are terrified of becoming a "BL." I was stumped. Not being fluent in initials, I had no idea what he was trying to tell me. "What?"

"Bag lady, women are all terrified of becoming bag ladies," he insisted.

I can't say I haven't thought about it and then immediately repressed it. I also can't say I haven't joked about the idea with friends and he's right, they've all been women. Shouldn't this be an equal opportunity nightmare?

What are men afraid of? Personally, I think men are terrified of lying on the bathroom floor in the middle of the night clutching their chest with no one around to call an ambulance.

I recently had a man ask me what I would do if I found him face down in the bathroom. What kind of question was that? Face down is quick; no muss, no fuss and no agonizing over what belongings will fit in the shopping cart and whether you should relocate to better weather. Thank God, I don't have a lot of stuff to put in the cart. Shoes might pose a problem, as there is no pair I can live without, especially if I'm in a temperate climate. I could wear my suede Kate Spades year round and those fab little Prada sling backs. Who am I kidding — shoes don't make the cut, but art does. I can't leave my art collection. I'll be the "BL" pushing a cart spilling over with art and a large Cindy Sherman photo rattling along the ground behind me.

I do know what one man is afraid of. He confided in me that he was afraid of "not being loved." Wow. I was stopped in my tracks. That's quite an admission. It made me think. Maybe it's not the bathroom floor or the shopping cart that's the scariest after all, it's "NBL."

My New Life of Dating Guppies

MIDDLE AGE DATING SUCKS. The days of "there are plenty of fish in the sea" have turned into "there are approximately four guppies in a toxic pond, floating on their side."

Sadly, even dating guppies requires time and energy. I constantly bemoan how much effort it takes to get ready: shower, wash hair, blow dry, makeup, pick an outfit, shoes, and purse, to say nothing of the ever present dilemma—to shave or not to shave my legs. These days, that is saved for when I think there is a chance of having sex. I don't have to shop for razors very often.

There's a shit load of pre-date work and the reward is a complete stranger I met online. Of course, I would prefer to be fixed up by one of my friends but that never happens. The only place to get a date these days is on an internet site, which at best is a complete crapshoot. I hate to gamble but like to go out.

I pick and choose as carefully as I can, short of hiring a private investigator to prescreen for me. Lately however, the best part of dating cyber-men has been coming home and thinking up fun nicknames for them. My evenings have run the gamut from trying to stay awake to being taken on a dinner date without dinner. This could be depressing but for the joy of giving each of them a little pet name: Mr. Dinnerless Dinner Date, Mr. 1973, Mr. Sweat Pants are for the Gym, Mr. Wake Me when the Check Comes and Mr. Not Quite Divorced. This last nickname did not bring me joy.

Mr. Not Quite Divorced falls in the same category as being a little bit pregnant. I couldn't help but wonder if he forgot he was still married. His profile status said, "divorced." Although if he wrote "not quite divorced" he'd be alone a lot. I think Mr. Not Quite Divorced needs to come with a notarized letter from his almost ex-wife stating that unless hell freezes over she would never take him back as well as her version of why they are splitting up. This could save me time and razor blades. A "not quite divorced guppy" needs to swim in the "still married but miserable" pond.

Thankfully, I didn't shave my legs.

IV
Face Value

Win $3,000, a Trip to Paris, or Me

I FINALLY HAD TO FACE IT—no one wanted to fix me up. No matter how I begged, pleaded, threatened or bribed, the response was "I don't know anyone to fix you up with." Give me a break. Not one of my family members, friends or even my mailman (yes, I'm a loser and asked him) knew an unattached male? This couldn't be possible when half the adult population is divorced. The question that haunts me is, where is this half and how come no one knows them?

Times have changed. When I was in my twenties and lived in New York City, every time I walked out the door I got a date. Men were everywhere. It was like fishing in a stocked pond. Of course, my gorgeous Golden Retriever was a guy magnet, but my ego could take it. We were a package deal; love the dog, love me. It sure was fun being 24 years old in Manhattan.

Flash forward 35 years and we're talkin' a whole new story. I walk outside and I'm invisible, except to people asking for money or directions. My apologies to that old guy I sent north instead of south. Even my super model yellow Lab doesn't help.

I am so over. I was frantic to come up with something better than "do you know anyone to fix me up with?" I needed a new strategic marketing plan.

I decided to focus on bribery. I offered a $3,000 vacation to the person, including the mailman, who found me a long term man. What better investment than myself. I was convinced there was nothing like $$$$ to jolt my friends into action. Checkbook in hand, I went off to offer the vacay to my girl Bobbi. "What do you mean not enough money?" I practically spit out my mocha skim latte with extra foam hearing this. I didn't though; I couldn't afford to.

"No offense sweetie, but it doesn't really cover the kind of vacation I'm used to, besides I still don't know anyone. Gotta run and pick up the boys for soccer, then baseball, then dinner, homework, baths."

"Blah blah blah blah" was the bubble over my stymied head. I was shocked and despondent. What was I offering, chicken liver? Prison camp? I needed new friends with less income.

I was tenacious, like a bulldog on a pant leg, but bribery continued to fail at my entry-level number. Finally and with great trepidation, I ponied up a trip to Paris. If it were the George V Hotel that my friends wanted in exchange for a man, I would borrow the cash. I was an "upstart" company and all new businesses take out loans. I'd worry about bankruptcy later.

"Sorry kiddo, I just got back from Europe and I'm exhausted. Besides Mark and I don't know a single man." Hope she had a great trip but what about me?

"Nope, I wish I knew someone but I'm so busy with the kids."

"I never really meet anyone on my route except women."

Now what? Or, if not now, when? I was growing older by the minute; I needed help. Someone help me!

"Honey, how about one of those dating sites? Someone at the beauty shop told me that her niece's best friend's husband's brother met his wife that way." I hated the beauty shop tales my mother loved to weave. Her affinity for complete strangers always disturbed me.

"Sure Mom, whatever. I bet they're really happy, gotta go."

Could Mom be right or finally have a story with merit? A dating site sounded so desperate and lonely, yet, I was desperate and lonely. Besides, it was a hell of a lot cheaper than my bankrupting offer of Paris.

I was weak, a bit hypoglycemic, and had two glasses of a cheap California Cabernet when I finally relented and turned on my computer to find love. And who was staring back at me but Dr. Phil. I think I screamed. He was the new spokesperson for Match.com. He looked happy, but I was buzzed and he was bald. I began to feel a little dizzy and with my blood sugar level dropping rapidly a light bulb went off—if all else failed I could date Dr. Phil. After a few non-lucid moments of pondering whether or not he was my type, I put my spinning head down on the keyboard but not before I clicked "join now."

"I Do...At Least I Think I Do"

WEDDING CEREMONIES ARE NOT FOR THE FAINT OF HEART. I just went to my nephew's wedding and although it was in an idyllic setting with a handsome groom, gorgeous bride and a bunch of hotties as attendants, the vows were a downer. Those are some mighty weighty questions. Truthfully, they're a little frightening and not for the ambivalent. Does anyone really think seriously about the answers? Everyone just seems to blurt out "I do." There's never a, "let me go home and give it some more serious thought, but go ahead with the cocktail hour." According to the divorce rate, "I'm not sure" would be a good response, or "huh," or even, "you talkin' to me?"

"Do you take this person for richer or for poorer?" Come on be honest, no one wants poorer. Especially the young trophy bride with the old guy; she needs the question rephrased "do you take this man for richer or for richer?" She definitely has to have an out-clause if things get poorer. Alas, he's not completely stupid; there's a prenup. I wish they'd read that at the ceremony.

"In sickness and in health?" Now that's a little morbid. Who gets to be healthy, and is there good medical insurance? It's a long time until Medicare kicks in and even then, you could end up stuck at home playing nursemaid. Then there's the deal sealer, "as long as you both shall live." Ha! That's made liars out of half of us, hasn't it? But there is the outside chance that you could marry your divorce attorney. I confess, I've lied twice and I consider myself honest. I'm not sure there is a good answer to that and probably should be eliminated to avoid perjury or hold up the ceremony.

I have to stay away from weddings as they confuse me. "I do, I don't, I'm not sure, maybe, I think I do for now, but maybe not later." Those are all reasonable answers and demand serious consideration.

Woodstock — The Wonder Years

"By the time we got to Woodstock we were half a million strong and everywhere was a song and a celebration."
—Joni Mitchell, Woodstock

DAMN, THE 40TH ANNIVERSARY of Woodstock has come and gone; am I that old? I just glanced in a mirror and the answer is "yes" and "geez." I am growing my hair long again, and absolutely, I think middle-aged women can have long hair no matter what they say on the morning talk shows. I probably won't be wearing bell-bottoms any time soon regardless of their being back in style. Now that's a really bad look over 50 and has anyone noticed how expensive blue jeans are? I could have a case of a lovely sauvignon blanc for the same price. The wine wins.

Sex, drugs, and rock and roll baby, remember? Was Woodstock the "good old days?" I'll be honest and — trust me — this is hard to confess, but I would no longer want to be drenching wet for three days, sleeping on the hard ground, peeing in a bush, and stuck in traffic for 12 hours even if Jimi Hendrix and Janis Joplin personally invited me to come. Is there any of the hippie chick left in me? However, I recently searched every street fair between Seattle and Portland for a tie dyed hoodie. Hippie or slave to fashion? As for drugs, pass the Advil. Or is your drug of choice Aleve? And for God's sake, turn the music down. I like quiet. I've become a loser by my own standards!

As for sex, those hippie boys sure were cute with their ponytails, flat abs and tight low riding jeans. It didn't take much imagination to picture having sex with one of them. Now I sit across from a date at dinner and visualizing sex ruins a perfectly good piece of Chilean Sea Bass and begs at least two martinis. Sadly, I look at him and realize hearing and being able to drive at night is the new "hip."

I Climbed Mt Everest in My Kate Spade High Heels

I HAD A FANTASY ABOUT CLIMBING MT. EVEREST. I hate the cold, detest the sight of snow and have a fear of heights but I could still dream.

"Chirp, chiiiiirrrrp, CHIRRRRRPP!" Holy crap, what was going on? I bolted up in bed and wildly looked around the room for a bird that must be loose. I checked the clock; it was 3:02 a.m. My first instinct was to burst into tears and my second was the same thing but that wouldn't stop the incessant chirping. Did I need a net or a gun? Having neither, I summoned my trusty yellow Lab to go hunting with me; after all, he's a bird dog and we had work to do. I wondered if boxer shorts and a t-shirt were proper attire.

Down the stairs we traipsed, trying to find the source of the shrill, hideous noise. I'm cursing, the dog's half asleep and not on the scent. "Potato, where's the bird, get him boy, go hunt."

He laid down and fell asleep in the living room while I stood there trying to track the chirp. It was directly over my head but it wasn't flying. It was a round white object—the smoke detector. Crap. The battery must have been low, but I was much lower, approximately 10 feet lower. I stared up at it with venom in my eyes. I had to stop it or be driven stark, raving mad. Chirp, chirp, chirp!

"Shut up," I screamed for no reason other than it made me feel proactive.

There was no ladder so I had to make do with a chair. I scaled the chair in my bare feet and reached up. I was 2' 8" away from peace and quiet. Now what? I needed more elevation—fast. A fat phone book seemed like a solution. I set the book on the chair and up I went. Damn, I wasn't even close. Two phone books had to do the trick. Nope, I still couldn't reach the freaking thing. Three phone books? I was getting dizzy and my tower of books was shaking but I was closer. Chirp. Right in my face as if to taunt my effort. Why wasn't I taller?

Then, an aha moment. I ran upstairs and put on my cute Kate Spade raspberry red, 3-inch suede high heels. I knew I'd wear them someday! Fortunately, no one saw me in my climbing attire: striped boxer shorts, ratty white t-shirt and heels. Look away or turn to stone!

With trepidation yet determination, I scaled the phone books. I had no climbing ropes mind you, or anything stable to hold onto. There I was solo, in peril, teetering on top of my man-made Mt. Everest. I barely got my hand around the chirping monster and yanked it off the ceiling. Victory was mine and I did it without Sherpas.

I put the detector on the counter and started to trundle back to my warm cozy bed.

"Chirp…chiiirp…CHIRP!" I was going insane. How could this be happening? There it sat on the counter with no battery, yet still chirping at me. I picked it up and held it in my hand, tears streaming down my face.

"Chirp, chirp."

Was I in Edgar Allen Poe's *The Tell-Tale Heart*? I was tired and broken. My only remaining solution was to get it out of the house. I dragged myself out to my car, threw it on the front seat and slammed the door. Silence.

As I trudged back upstairs feeling victorious and like a latter day Sir Edmond Hillary, I realized I had fulfilled my dream of climbing Mt. Everest. Remarkably, I did it in a pair of raspberry red, Kate Spade high heels and without supplemental oxygen.

Right on, Mom!

MOM'S TURNING 100! Holy crap, how did she do it? And why after all these years of silence about her age, was she confessing to such a huge number?

Growing up, I had no idea how old she was. In fact, I think she had three birth certificates and four driver's licenses all with different dates of birth. I don't believe any of those documents were correct but I was impressed with her craftiness. Regardless of this high level of secrecy, she was mortified she would be found out. I confess my sister and I rummaged through her drawers once for a birth certificate to no avail. We did find $10 and split it.

Mother came by her deceptive ways honestly, as her mother, aka Nana, carried on these covert operations also. My mom never knew the exact age of her Mom. The closest approximation we came to when she died was 85 or 110, or possibly 93.

Nana was a thinker. She had real skills to cover her tracks. Brilliantly, she lied about her children's ages. And like good soldiers they obeyed her orders. My mother carried on this time-honored tradition and didn't tell the truth about her daughters' ages either. I've lied for so long I've forgotten the real number. Amnesia is a blessing.

So why confess at 100? She's defied the aging process and could easily hang out at 85 for years to come. There are days I stare at her and think she looks a hell of a lot better than I do. It's depressing. In a test of who has the better jawline, she'd win hands down. When I realized this, I burst into tears.

Mom is a walking testimonial to every makeup counter at Neimans, Saks and Bloomingdales. Sisley products have taken on religious significance. If you're lost and looking for purpose or something in which to believe, there is a facial mask for that.

I Am Not a Bar Loser Anymore

PICK-UP BARS WERE NEVER MY IDEA of a way to spend an evening. If I did go out with my friends, I brought a book because men never cozied up to me. I was brunette. My girlfriends were blondes. They got all the attention and I was shoved out of the way on the race to get to them. So there I was, the lone brunette with my head down, reading. This actually was ok with me because I never took "bar speak" which I think consists mostly of monosyllables. I didn't develop the fine art of idle chitchat. My lightest subject was films by Truffaut. I was alone a lot. Every once in a while a guy would ask me what I was reading and I'd look up long enough to say "I love Salinger, do you?" Conversation over. Bars made me nervous and sweaty.

I spent no time between college and the present going to bars to meet the opposite sex. Unfortunately being single again after two marriages, I find myself facing that option. My skills, however, remain at bringing reading material.

Now it's mostly the New York Times, which in an area as conservative and Republican as Palm Desert, California leaves me alone on my bar stool.

I am also still brunette in the land of blondes and relatively flat chested in a sea of cleavage. I made a brief attempt at becoming partially blonde and buying a push up bra but apparently didn't fool anyone because I got a lot of reading done. I resigned myself to the fact that I was a bar loser.

It was a Saturday night when my lonely bar life changed. I went to "The Nest" in Palm Desert, known for being the hottest, oldest and most raucous pick-up place in a 100-mile radius. I'm talking old, as the male demographic is probably 60 to 95 years. And those 95-year olds loved me. Every bad toupee looked my way regardless of my brown hair and lack of cleavage. Even the comb overs were winking at me. I walked by a man who was asleep at a table and he woke up to check me out. I had no time to read or talk about foreign films as I was getting hit on from every direction.

My head was spinning. I danced with a man who just had a knee and hip replaced; he was a real trier but unsteady and might have broken my little toe. I think a guy in a multi-colored sweater tried to sell me a cemetery plot but it was so noisy I could hardly hear him. I'm not exactly sure but I could have sworn I saw a man come out of the bathroom juggling a bottle of Viagra but it could have been Prevacor. The joint was jumping. I went from bar loser to the big time in no time. I was a legend in my own mind.

I might go back, but first I have to get my toe x-rayed.

A Little Dab'll Do Ya

I HATE WHEN I WALK INTO A DEPARTMENT STORE and the first thing that happens is sales people rushing towards me spraying bottles of perfume. "No, no, go away. Please, no perfume, it makes my eyes turn red and burn." I frantically wave my hands in the air and run to the shoe department where my olfactory senses are safe. My wallet is now in danger but I've spared my vision. I never ever wear perfume, or at least not since high school when I would douse myself in Shalimar. I can't help but wonder if that became a banned substance or an ingredient in Agent Orange.

I had a Match.com date recently who defied the laws of "a little dab'll do ya." I sat down to have a drink with him in a local restaurant and was engulfed in a noxious cloud of cologne. I think I went blind for a second. He smiled, and I tried not to have a seizure. Why were his eyes not red and watery but crystal clear, and why were they staring at my twitching upper lip? I had no idea how long I could sit there without grabbing the nearest fire extinguisher and hosing him down. Was the desire to coat himself in a foreign odor an evolutionary instinct so as to separate him from the apes? (And before that evening I would never date an ape, which I might now rethink.) Or could the act of swimming in cologne be an animal rite of sexual passage to insure fertility? Whatever it is, I was dying.

I am not one to up and leave after ten minutes, regardless of a Match.com mismatch, and I have never used the pretend emergency phone call from a friend. So I stayed; all I could do was take shallow breaths of air and drink. He was a nice guy who happily showed me lovely pictures of his African safari and shared news of his upcoming surgery which interested me more than another date with him. I politely opted out of a second glass of wine as I felt like my eyes were on fire and I was becoming asthmatic. He offered me a ride home because I had walked to the restaurant, but I was terrified of getting in his car, as being in an enclosed space would definitely ensure my having to take a shower strong enough to remove plutonium.

I walked home rethinking my Match.com profile and decided to state that I was searching for a cologne-free man or a primate.

R.I.P My Prada Purse

I LOVE MY PURSE. MY PRADA BAG goes with me everywhere and is one of my prize possessions. It is simple, beautiful, a leathery work of art and I did not pay retail for it. That would have required a bank loan or second mortgage. Fabulous and on sale, it was a dream come true. Sadly, regardless of my coddling and caretaking, it is dying. My Prada bag is fading fast. The corners are ripping badly and no one can save it. I've thrown myself sobbing on the counters of shoemakers and saddle repair people from Chicago to Southern California begging them to bring my bag back to life but alas, no one has hope.

"Please save my precious Prada bag. Don't let it die." Its days are numbered and loose change will be falling out of the corners very soon. With dread in my heart, I have to find a new love.

I thought my mother, the Imelda Marcos of purses, might be able to console me in my despair. I don't understand why she needs so many as I love only one.

"Mom, what could possibly go with this?" I queried as I pulled a chartreuse leather clutch off a shelf in her closet.

"You know I forgot I had that, but I must say when I bought it the color was very popular. It was from Neimans." She snatched the purse out of my hands as if I would somehow damage it. There were so many piled up in her closet I had to save her from a large black purse falling on her head.

"Oh I love that bag, it's a Fendi you know," she remarked as I grabbed it out of the air.

No, I didn't know, as I'm not in the purse "know."

"Do you want it dear, it's a Fendi," she repeated as if I didn't understand the significance of her offer. "They are very expensive." Once again, she repeated she bought it at Neimans.

Mom must be the Warren Buffet of their purse department. Her Fendi bag was bigger than my yellow Lab and for that matter, my mother. "No thanks, you keep it," I said, my head hung in handbag despair. It paled to my Prada.

I turned to my friend Adria for help. She told me she has approximately 75 purses. "Oh I rotate them with my winter and summer clothes. I have to bring the purse bins up and down from the basement every season."

Excuse moi? Bins? Filled with purses? I was way behind the handbag curve in my peer group. I loved only one and she had bins. I felt desperately confused and wondered if there was anything more I could do to prolong the life of my Prada bag. Where will I go, what will I do and how much will it cost me? I fear it is only a matter of days until I will have to venture forth to Neimans, Nordstrom's, Bloomingdales, Saks and perhaps as far as Bergdorfs to find love again and hoping my mother passed on a gene marked "handbag."

I Look Better in Dim Lighting

I JUST READ AN ARTICLE THAT ASSURED ME that I would never be too old to look young. Plastic surgery is on the rise for septuagenarians, octogenarians and even nonagenarians. (If you know what "nonagenarian" means without using "dictionary.com," I'll send you a gift bag.) This is good news for my mom, who actually is a nonagenarian. She is always looking in the mirror and shocked by her wrinkles. "Wow Mom, if I live to be your age I'll be shocked I still have a reflection."

The good news for Mom is that it's not too late for her to look 88 again as 84,685 surgical procedures were done on patients over 65 in just one calendar year. It's true no one wants to age gracefully and cheaply. With folks living longer and remaining healthier, they want their bodies in alignment with their mentality. Truthfully, I'm not sure any surgeon could make me look 18.

Are you tired of your slackened jowls, flabby underarms, droopy eyelids, turkey neck, gravity defying breasts or mile-wide thighs? Well don't despair, it's not too late no matter what your age to just say "no" to your body. I have learned that older patients may take longer to heal and the results of plastic surgery may not last as long as in a younger patient, but isn't it worth your 401k to look 20 years younger for a month or two? I don't know about you but I'm sick of living in dim lighting. I want to uncover the mirrors. And I want to stop asking the maître d' for the table back in the corner.

Thankfully, this news gives me years to decide what to do with my face. Should I take the plunge and hope to look like I'm in my late forties again or wait another 15 years and ironically be thrilled to look exactly how I look now?

Collecting Husbands and Stamps

I'VE HAD TWO HUSBANDS, which at one time seemed like a lot. I have, however, met men and women who are on their third, fourth and fifth spouse. It's a little jaw dropping but seeing as how everyone is living so much longer, it's apparently possible to collect marriages like stamps. (Btw, does anyone actually collect stamps anymore?)

I feel thankful I got married in the 1970s and then again in the 80's as I never would have met either husband in 2017. It is necessary to LOOK UP to meet someone. Has anyone else noticed that everyone is looking down texting or talking on his or her cell phone? Truthfully, I'm shocked more folks haven't walked into oncoming traffic or trains. Everywhere I go, men and women are yapping away on their phones, probably complaining they never go out. Wake up, all you 21st century dateless whiners—get a 20th century answering machine and leave the cell phone at home.

I admit this is much easier said than done but let me take you back to yesteryear. I met husband #1 in an age when phones plugged into a wall. The year was 1976 and the place, Central Park. I was walking my golden retriever and he was out with his golden retriever. The dogs started playing and we started chitchatting. Now if either one of us had been on a cell phone or texting we would never have looked up long enough to have a conversation. I would have been on my tiny device bitching and moaning to a friend how I was dateless and my future husband would have gotten away.

Husband #2 was trickier but again, I was looking up. I was meeting my friend Ellen at the Museum of Modern Art when I realized I was $1.00 short of the admission price. (Foolishly, I couldn't resist a purse in the window of the Coach store on the way over.) Panicked, I knew I had to borrow money from a total stranger to get in. It was 1984 and phones were still attached to walls, so no texting or calling her about my cash shortage. I looked around the lobby and decided if I had to make a complete fool of myself and beg for money I might as well pick the best looking man in sight. Voila! I got the $1.00 and another husband. Yes, I paid him back.

It's 2018 and I find myself spending a lot of time looking down texting or talking and complaining about my paltry dating life. Obviously, I am not taking my own advice. I am so far behind the marital curve that I would have to live to 120 to get up to three or four ex-spouses. Truthfully, I think there's only one answer. I'll collect stamps.

My First Kiss: Fact or Fiction?

DO YOU REMEMBER YOUR FIRST KISS? I do. Or I thought I did. I would have testified in a court of law, taken a lie detector test or bet my firstborn that my first real kiss was from Doug Simmons. I'm embarrassed to admit that it didn't happen until high school, as I was way behind on kissing. There was a lot of kissing going on in middle school, just not with me. I was slow dancing but not kissing. It wasn't until freshman year that I found myself in the "Oh my God, I think he's going to kiss me" position. I was so nervous.

Mr. First Kiss was adorable. I had a crush on him but never thought he'd reciprocate as he was an upper classman and hung out with cheerleaders. How I longed to be a cheerleader as that was the surefire route to popularity and kissing. Unfortunately, I wasn't perky enough and truthfully, this white girl couldn't jump.

I remember everything about that kiss. Doug drove me over to his house after school in his sexy little sports car, which dazzled me. He took my hand and we walked around back to his swimming pool; the setting was very "Town and Country." Then in one instant as we stood by the pool he leaned down and kissed me. A moment I will never forget but a kiss I would. "Is this it? This is what all the hoopla is about? This is kissing on the lips? "Ewwww" was the bubble over my head. I didn't chip any teeth, which was a blessing because they were finally straight from years of braces. My lip wasn't bleeding either which was good, as it could have stained the collar on my new Villager blouse. We never kissed again.

And that's the story of my first kiss, or so I thought. There is now evidence to the contrary. All the years of believing my first kiss was Doug Simmons has been challenged. Harry Levin has come forward out of the blue and claimed that he kissed me on a golf course at a Bar Mitzvah party in 8th grade. Au contraire I declared, but he begged to differ and, making matters more confusing, he stated that he could produce a witness. Jonathan Teller apparently was there and saw him kiss me, which is kind of "Peeping Tom-ish" but also very CSI.

Was my first kiss memory a myth? I have no "Town and Country" sexy sports car story if Harry is right. It will take a period of adjustment and perhaps therapy to come to terms with the fact that my first kiss was really my second.

Fractured Fairy Tale

MY MOTHER GOOFED AGAIN. Granted she was busy at the makeup counter of Saks, and shopping the sales at Bloomingdales but this information would really have helped me out.

I hate hearing "pearls of wisdom" from a woman half my age on the Today Show. This makes morning programming too much like televangelism instead of background noise. I peeked my head out from behind my computer upon hearing, "Three out of four women will be widowed by age 75." Very bad news for a lot of men out there and sucked for me also if I had any hopes of marrying again.

She went on to "preach" that women should wed for love and not as a financial alternative. Now that's novel, and Mom, you were wrong. This is interesting information that came about 35 years too late for me. She also went on to say that I should be actively involved in financial planning as I could end up a poor widow or just plain poor and alone. I'm a little panicky because I rejoined Match.com, which set me back $70 that I should have invested in the stock market or lottery tickets. The double whammy is, even if I meet someone he'll be dead soon. I ran to the closet to make sure I had a black dress.

I can't blame it all on Mom, and my obsession with Cinderella. I was from the generation of women on the brink, so close to reality and yet so far. I wasn't raised to work. I don't know what I was supposed to do with my time but it wasn't earn money. If Mom was my role model, I was supposed to spend my husband's money. A reasonable plan with good perks like a new car, charge cards, weekly hair appointments, clothes and a maid. Career woman was an option still a few years away. I only got as far as birth control pills, bra burning, and political protests. I quit taking the pill when they determined they could cause strokes, my breasts are no longer defying gravity so I need the bra, but political protests are making a comeback and I am skilled in this area.

With no words from Mom about how to support myself, I married a rich man and thought I solved the problem. But let's not place the onus all on Mom; after all Dad had a career, and could have mentioned the "c" word as something I might want to consider. Did he just forget?

I have a career now; it took two divorces and two questionably small divorce settlements to shock me into the work force. I parlayed art collecting into art advising and selling. Although starting so late, I will have to work until about ten minutes before I die. Since I don't have a daughter, I didn't have the chance to instill in her more than the Prince Charming option; a storybook that would have been banned from my household along with the movie *Pretty Woman*. I probably would have sent her off to medical, law, dental, business and veterinary school, just to make sure she could buy her own horse and not have to rely on the Prince.

Mom, it's not your fault for not sending me to the aforementioned professional schools. I was terrible at chemistry so it was never in my future regardless. You only wanted the best for me, and thought a husband should provide it. I hope, however, my $70.00 Match.com membership is refundable. I need lottery tickets.

Prune Danish

I'M SURE THERE ARE A LOT OF PEOPLE happier than I am, but it's hard to believe they're all in Denmark. Yep, it's true; it's the world's happiest country. It seems impossible to me as they have snow. And it's cold there. Why aren't they miserable? Maybe weather hasn't been elevated to the status of life-threatening danger like it has here in Chicago. Maybe they don't realize they're freezing and depressed. Maybe their local weather person isn't a failed drama major screaming, "a storm is coming, two feet of snow by morning, don't drive, stay home until the roads are clear, hopefully by next week," like mine is. "Shut up," I scream back at the TV, tears streaming down my face. This is not happiness in my book.

Hey Danish people, what about Hamlet? He wasn't cheerful; in fact he was downright morose, tortured and confused with a questionable love life. Are you not factoring him in? Has the play been confiscated from your theaters, libraries, and banned from school curriculums to help lighten the mood? I suggest you replace it with *Death of a Salesman* to see what you're all really made of.

According to the news, Danish people don't aspire to the Great American Dream. I'm sure this is a mood booster as it really only leads to perpetual dissatisfaction. Seriously, without my expectation of a six-figure income, Viking stove, S Class Mercedes and whirlwind weekends in Paris, waking up in a small one-bedroom apartment might be fun. I wonder if Americans would be happier if we weren't obsessed with erectile dysfunction, flat abs, wrinkles and perpetual youth. Is there a woman alive who would feel delighted if her husband or lover had an erection that lasted more than four hours? Let me know if you are out there and what medication you're taking.

Danes also have royalty, so lovely and polite; perhaps this is a mood lifter. We have the Kardashians, so tasteless and embarrassing.

Danish people eat sardines. This could be the path to happiness. It just so happens I like them. Maybe I should forget the afternoon's mocha skim latte and dig into a sandwich of those slippery little creatures to lift my spirits.

I feel almost giddy.

I Want a Dog's Life

WHO WOULD TRADE THEIR DOG FOR A MAN? I'm guessing not many. Remember when Leona Helmsley left $12 million to her dog "Trouble"? It seemed extreme at the time, but now I realize it was excellent estate planning. Hey little furry guy, you're far better off than I am. No worrying about your doghouse going into foreclosure or whether you can afford health care. I assume you have a team of veterinarians. I hope you have a good accountant, however, as $12 million dollars doesn't go as far as it used to. Take it easy on the chauffeur bills, and no more canary yellow diamond collars. If you get lonely and want a new owner, however, I'm available.

I've had men and dogs in my life. Each dog outlasted a husband. It was never really a tough call. Congratulations to Jonah and Miami, my golden retriever and yellow Lab who survived Stuart and Bucky. Also a big shout out to Thurber, my doberman who trumped three long-term relationships.

They were great dogs and ironically, it wasn't hard for any of them to learn "stay."

I love that dogs don't care about cooking. Isn't that great? Every day the same meal and not a peep out of them. My yellow Lab, Potato, thinks I am Julia Child the way he scarfs down his food. He also seems perfectly happy listening to me complain about everything. He likes my choice of TV shows and politics. I love that he thinks I'm nice, unlike most people, to say nothing of his sleeping on the floor next to the bed instead of hogging it. I admit I'm envious of his hair color but resist the temptation to go blonde.

The decision is a no brainer; it's the dog.

Why I Am Not a Cougar

I WISH I WAS A COUGAR but I don't have the chutzpah to hunt younger men. Cougars, how and where do you do this? I would love to track down 35-year-old boys with hair and flat abs.

"Google" defines you Cougars as over the age of 40, financially independent, successful, confident, motivated, loving your life and self. Are you having a membership drive or bake sale any time soon? Cougars survive on a tasty cuisine of men at least 10 years younger. Yummy and I'm feeling hungry.

Curiously, old men have preyed on younger women for years; they've been called "lucky" and not some form of wild mountain cat. Rumor has it younger men are more energetic, fun and trainable. The happy word is trainable, yet it sounds time consuming. I'm the lazy sort who always wonders when I get a new puppy why I just didn't buy a 2-year-old dog. No muss, no fuss, they sit, stay and don't pee on the rug. I prefer this in a man, also.

I dated younger and "trainable" once. He had all those good puppy qualities: cute, playful, energetic, youthful enthusiasm, stared at me adoringly and mindfully. Not bad, I'd say. Was I crazy to leave him? For starters, he never read one play by Shakespeare, one book by Hemingway or F. Scott Fitzgerald, stared vacantly at me when I mentioned Hunter Thompson, no less William Burroughs or Jack Kerouac. No *Catcher in the Rye* in his personal reading history, or *Annie Hall* or *Easy Rider*. Yes, there was a war in Vietnam and Watergate brought down a President named Nixon. "You were three when Kennedy was shot?" Crap, my puppy man and I had very different life landmarks. Sadly, those aren't trainable. The flat abs and full head of brown hair were nice, though.

I confess I really do like puppies and will probably have another one regardless of the paper training, accidental peeing on the rug, and the time consuming lessons of sit and stay. As for men—must come fully trained.

I Feel Bad About My Face and Neck

I JUST SPENT MY ENTIRE 401K on skin care products. I can't decide whether to faint or hang myself. The most I ever paid for moisturizer to date was $8.99 and now in my possession were two jars of cream more costly than my rent. Who does this? Maybe Beyonce or Lady Gaga, but not someone who is too cheap to take the tollway. I've obviously lost my mind and might lose my apartment if I have to decide between rent and paying for the costly products.

It was my sister's fault. It really feels better to blame someone. She let me try her new wonder products, and threatened my life if I dropped one of the jars. The sales girl told her it takes just a tiny dab of cream and voila, that dewy pre-menopausal complexion will return.

So Mother Nature, it may cost me, but I'm getting revenge. I triumphantly dabbed and stared in the mirror. "Come on, come on, I don't have all day!" Damn, no dewiness but my skin did feel soft.

"Soft" required a bank loan. I gasped as the woman behind the makeup counter at Neimans added up my bill. Oh God and the banks are so stingy lately. Should I call the Fed Chairman?

My girlfriends and I have determined facelifts don't make anyone look younger; they just make you look like you had a facelift. A sales lady at Saks told me one of her customers has had so many eye lifts she can no longer close one of them all the way. Ewwww. Btw, I agreed with Nora Ephron—"I hate my neck" also. (Don't suggest a turtleneck as it's only a short-term solution to a long-term problem.)

I've stuck my Neiman's charge card away in a drawer and put retirement on permanent hold. I have placed the jars of "miracle working" face and eye cream far away from the edge of the sink. I think I would have to be hospitalized if one broke. I'm dutifully dabbing and, of course, staring in the mirror. Sadly not much to report, other than buyer's remorse. I long for the good old days of $8.99 moisturizer and financial liquidity.

KISS ME! But Only if You Can

SEARCHING FOR A PERFECT GIFT for that special someone? I'm not, unless it costs $3.27. I have to face it, given my checking account, this year's gift giving is going to take some "thinking outside the box." Ever wonder what's inside the box and why it's never a good idea?

I read in the paper that one of the questions most asked on Google was "how to kiss." Wow, and really? Now granted, you can't wrap kissing lessons up in a pretty little package but if someone's a bad kisser, teaching them would be the greatest gift of all. Do Jimmy Carter and Bill Gates know about this kind of good will, as they are consummate philanthropists in my mind.

It's downright nerve-wracking wondering whether or not someone is going to be a good kisser. I've spent entire first dates sitting across from a man and while I might have been talking about movies, politics, or weather patterns, I was really only thinking about how he kisses. This is time consuming, anxiety provoking, usually gives me a headache and sometimes hives. Good kisser? Bad kisser? Good kisser, bad kisser? I haven't heard a word he's said, nor cared. Then my, "Oh please let him be a good kisser prayer" kicks in. How great would it be if this worry was eradicated? No more anxiety, just joy and relaxation knowing everyone was a good kisser.

But the bad kissers are still out there. It's really sad when the big first kiss is just about to happen, the moment I've focused on all night, the anticipation building, my head pounding, the prayer endlessly running through my brain and my cute date gets closer, closer, ever closer. The time has finally arrived and then "Oh no, oh no, bad, bad, bad, what is he doing?" I think he chipped my front tooth! No, not a drooler! He's ruining my new dress. I need a dentist and 24-hour dry cleaner.

I desperately tried to teach someone to be a better kisser. If you think it's quick and easy, you're wrong. I worked diligently at it. Believe me, it wasn't fun or sexy and my TMJ flared up, but it was better kissing or so long mister. Finally, after four or five failed attempts I threw in the towel as he never caught on to the nuances of a really great kiss and I couldn't afford chipped teeth or a night guard for my jaw.

I definitely need to get in touch with Bill Gates or Jimmy Carter.

Me and the Prince of Denmark

"TO SLEEP, PERCHANCE TO DREAM." Hold on, wacky Prince of Denmark; if you could fall asleep, why can't I? I don't have nearly as much on my mind as you did. I also have mother issues—but not as serious as yours—and I'm wide awake.

My mom wants to know what I'm wearing, where I'm going and who I'm with. She's also obsessed with a facial mask I should apply for my wrinkles but I'm sure your Mom wasn't as pesky about appearances. Of course, you also weren't worried about a mortgage because you lived in a castle that was paid for. No foreclosures in your world. I'm guessing you didn't have the rising cost of health care about which to wrack your brain, or the nagging dilemma of, to get a colonoscopy or not to get a colonoscopy. No wonder I can't sleep.

What happened to the days when I woke up at the crack of noon? Granted I was 17 but I had stress then also. Was my blue Villager sweater back from the cleaners, and did

Roger like me or Joby? I forgot to finish my algebra homework because I couldn't figure out the difference between x and y. On a more serious note, did my parents notice the car smelled from cigarettes and beer? Sadly, I wasn't invited to the Senior Prom but had a dress picked out; now that was true tragedy and gave me pimples. Last and really tragic, I forgot about applying to college.

Those were real sleep busters, but regardless I dozed off. I was dreaming like that wacky Prince. I was crushed, yet sleepy. Now I listen to the commercials for sleep aids and try to come up with new ways to coerce my doctor into another prescription for Ambien. I long for sleep and oddly, my blue Villager sweater. (P.S—Roger liked Joby)

Botox or Bust?

GOT BOTOX? I DO NOT. But I'm thinking about it. I was in California where the wrinkle producing sun may have been out all the time but the women have smooth skin and nice plumped up lips. Last time I looked in the mirror I let out a gasp and started noticeably sweating. I think even my unconscious was frightened. I spent some quality time staring at my forehead and noticed it furrowed a lot. I look chronically worried.

Is facial expression passé? A syringe full of magic paralytic agents and presto-chango no wrinkles or look of terror on my face. Not one teenie weenie twitch, which is creepy *and* awesome! No one would have a clue as to what I was thinking, which really would help me have more friends.

I watched my mom at the front lines of fighting age when I was growing up. Her rituals were painstaking and time consuming. A veritable arsenal of creams, lotions, potions, wands and masks were her weapons to combat wrinkles. At the time I thought she was nuts. I screamed when she came near me with her slimy smelly moisturizers. Even today with no help from paralytic injections, plumper-uppers or a surgeon's scalpel, she's still fighting. "Never surrender" is her battle cry while mine is "I give up."

Trying to look young again is hard work. Personally, I feel defeated and want to burst into tears. I'm exhausted running from mirror to mirror trying to determine which one makes me look better. I think it's the one in the guest bedroom and I decide to live there.

What happened to growing old gracefully? I'm growing old and don't know what to do.

I'm torn between grace and Botox.

Ken Dolls Grow Old, Too

HAPPY 45TH BIRTHDAY, KEN DOLL! Welcome to middle age, plastic guy. Time flies, doesn't it? I couldn't celebrate Barbie's big 50 and ignore your day. Kudos to Barbie for being cutting edge and dating a younger man way before it was hip. Right on, blondie!

Personally, Ken was never my type. He had bad clothes and although I desperately wanted to be a cheerleader, I never wanted to date one. No megaphone boys for me. He also had felt hair that fell off when wet. "Oh my God Ken, your hair's at the bottom of the pool!" That must have been a big turn-off for our little Barbie in her itsy bitsy bikini. I know I would have dumped him after I stopped screaming.

Did anyone know the plastic fantastic duo broke up in 2004? What could possibly have split them up when they seemed so perfect? Was Ken in full midlife crisis? Poor Barbie wasn't a young hottie anymore? Ken, wake up you dope; she still had perky breasts, a wrinkle-free forehead, and a great colorist. Did plastic boy buy a Porsche and start wearing Eurotrash clothing from Barneys while our girl was training hard to be an astronaut, nurse and Olympian?

Don't fret blondie, there's always GI Joe. He must be out of the armed forces by now with a very nice pension. Hopefully, he's ditched the camouflage clothes, purchased some civilian outfits and still has hair and flat abs.

As for Ken, cheerleaders never age well.

Dressing for Successful Dating

I'M AN UNCONCERNED DRESSER. I get up in the morning, throw gym shorts and a hoodie on over the boxer shorts and t-shirt in which I slept and think I'm presentable. It's a little scary but quick and also requires no thinking. Truthfully, I'm in this snappy outfit until around noon. If I do have to go anywhere, I usually put on jeans and a short or long sleeved t-shirt depending on the weather. Not a fashion statement but again, mindless.

My mother, on the flipside, spends half the day going from closet to closet to closet deciding what to wear. This includes her shoe, purse and jewelry selection. I did not inherit these genes or impulses. When I visit her, she stares at what I'm wearing and asks me if I want a piece of her clothing as a gift. It usually includes a cape. "No Mom, I hate capes," I declare every time but she never remembers.

My laissez-faire attitude towards dressing makes going on a date difficult, coupled with the problem that unlike

Mom I only have one closet and it is half-full. My friend Adria can attest to this as she stood in front of it one day screaming, "No self-respecting Jewish Princess would have so little clothing."

My deepest apologies to all the women that I've failed. I know better than to go on a date in my gym shorts and hoodie so I have my work cut out for me when it comes time to get ready. It's hard to keep my head from exploding.

Saturday night, it took six outfit changes to get out the door. A white V-neck shirt with black skirt and little gray jacket was my initial instinct. Wrong jacket and the skirt looked weird with the t-shirt. I flung it off. The black skirt with black top and black blazer I tried would only work if we were eating at a funeral home. Off it went. Little black cocktail dress? Nope, too dressy. Frustrated, I tossed it on the bed. Skinny jeans with white shirt and black blazer. Very SoHo, but not exactly right. I threw the shirt across the room; it landed on the dog who looked better in it than I did but also dizzy from watching the flying clothes.

I was close to tears but not close to dressed. I rummaged through the remaining things in my closet but it all became one black blur and I was running late. Desperately I pulled out a tight black V-neck shirt, and put the skinny jeans and black blazer back on. Not bad—understated chic yet a touch too morbid. I no longer cared. I gave thumbs up to the dog who followed me to the front door with the t-shirt draped on his head. I groaned as I stared back at the clothes strewn all over my room and couldn't help but wonder if dating was worth the cleanup.

Dance of the Seven Plungers!

"THEY JUST DON'T MAKE THINGS THE WAY THEY USED TO."

Who said that? It couldn't have been me; I'm too young, too hip, too cool and recently decided to be brunette again. Old people sit around and grouse about such things; I don't. I'm convinced I'm too young to know how they used to make stuff. My dad says things like that. Oh God, I've become my dad. Quick get the meds. I'm kvetching about the good old days—who am I? I need an emergency trip to Saks to get refocused. My mom doesn't care about the way things are made as long as they cost a lot. I want to be her.

I had an "old person" day of reckoning; I'm here to say that they don't make plungers the way they used to. And yes, every household still needs a plunger regardless of whether you Facebook, Tweet, Snapchat, Instagram or use the latest version of an iPhone.

I am willing to admit that I'm a domestic loser. I was cleaning the toilet with one of those cloth things that are on a wand. Now I ask you, why do they have a release button if you can't flush the "thing" part down the damn toilet? No sooner had I released and flushed than I knew it would never make it. "No, come back, I goofed, don't go. I'm a household loser."

I ran for the plunger. I could save the day and the need for a costly plumber. Ready, plunge! My plunger turned inside out like a cheap umbrella. It did not snap back into place and was useless. Useless I say! The water was rising and my flimsy plunger remained inside out on a stick. I specifically remember the plungers from my childhood did not do this. I was freaking out so I ran to the basement and found another one. It was gross but better than my house needing FEMA agents. Again—ready, aim, plunge! Damn, who makes these things, General Motors? "I hate you," I screamed and ran out the door.

I had to take matters into my own hands. Ace Hardware, plumbing aisle was my first stop. I ripped one off the shelf and practiced plunged. Yep, inside out, another fake. Was the world coming to an end? I flung it back and hightailed it to the car. Home Depot loomed on the horizon. If not there, where? I put my head on the shoulder of the man in charge of plumbing equipment and sobbed about the good old days of heavy duty rubber plungers. He understood. He gently placed two types in my hands and told me one was a new plastic contraption that would never bring me happiness and the other exactly what I was looking for. I practiced plunged for 15 minutes and he was right, it snapped back every time. I stopped crying, thanked him, promised to send my friends to his aisle, and maybe flowers on Father's Day.

I arrived home victorious with my real rubber, good old-fashioned plunger. Neimans has never brought me that kind of joy.

I Need a Push-up Bra

DAMN. I MISSED THE "COUGAR" CONVENTION that was held right here in Chicago. It could have filled some of the long holiday weekend. Instead of worrying about getting corn on the cob stuck between my teeth or choking on a hot dog and no one knowing the Heimlich maneuver, I could have stood in front of my closet and fretted over the fact I didn't have a dress low cut enough to attract a "cub." A what, you ask? I learned watching a news feed about the event that a "cub" is a man under forty. The Cougar women are hunting for little cubbies. They sure looked cute, fit, trim, sexy and smiley. Who wouldn't want one; they're like puppies. "I'll take that one and that one and that shy one in the corner." It's like ordering from the Neiman Marcus Christmas catalogue, only better and cheaper.

I don't know if I have what it takes to be a Cougar. I think a push-up bra is a staple. It is also necessary to have something to push up. My mom recently asked when we were out shopping, "Gail, what happened to your breasts? I remember you used to have them." Is there a right answer to that question?

I also noticed the Cougar women wore a lot of makeup, which looked nice but uh oh. I've never had the patience or mental fortitude to look in the mirror long enough to apply much makeup. In fact, these days I try to do it fast and with my eyes closed. Then there's the wardrobe issue. How many low cut dresses would I need to catch a cub and can you also wear them to the gym?

The convention really looked like fun; everyone was drinking and laughing. I hate cash bars however, so if you had to pay over $5.00 for a drink I would have been cranky, sulky and not smiley enough to attract a cub. It was better to stay home and get a puppy.

Made in the USA
Middletown, DE
08 April 2019